IN THE BEGINNING

there was a book written by Terry Pratchett and Neil Gaiman about the forces of good and evil coming together to prevent the apocalypse, scheduled to happen on a Saturday just after tea.

Now, that internationally beloved novel has been transformed into six hour-long episodes of some of the most creative and ambitious television ever made. Written and show-run by Neil Gaiman and directed by Douglas Mackinnon, this BBC Studios creation brings *Good Omens* spectacularly to life, through a cast that includes Michael Sheen, David Tennant, Jon Hamm, Miranda Richardson, Josie Lawrence, Derek Jacobi, Nick Offerman, Jack Whitehall and Adria Arjona.

Keep calm, because *The Nice and Accurate Good Omens TV Companion* is your ultimate guide to navigating Armageddon. Through character profiles and in-depth interviews with the stars and the crew, stunning behind-the-scenes and stills photography of the cast and locations, and a fascinating insight into costume boards and set designs, you will discover the feats of creativity and mind-boggling techniques that have gone into bringing an angel, a demon and the Antichrist to the screens of people everywhere. This book will take you inside the world of Heaven and Hell (and Tadfield) and is set to shatter coffee tables around the world.

The Nice and Accurate

GOOD OMENS

TV Companion

The Nice and Accurate

GOOD OMENS

TV Companion

Your guide to Armageddon
and the series based on the bestselling novel by
Terry Pratchett and Neil Gaiman

By Matt Whyman

HEADLINE

Printed and bound in China by C&C Offset
Colour reproduction by AltaImage UK
Design by Lynnette Eve at Design Jam
Project Management by Emma Tait

All quotes from the *Good Omens* script are taken from Neil Gaiman's read-through script © BBC
Every effort has been made to fulfill requirements with regard to reproducing copyright material.
The author and publisher will be glad to rectify any omissions at the earliest opportunity.

Headline's policy is to use papers that are natural, renewable and recyclable products and
made from wood grown in sustainable forests. The logging and manufacturing processes are
expected to conform to the environmental regulations of the country of origin.

HEADLINE PUBLISHING GROUP
An Hachette UK Company
Carmelite House
50 Victoria Embankment
London EC4 0DZ
www.headline.co.uk
www.hachette.co.uk

All images by Christopher Raphael © BBC except the following: Claire Anderson / Sophie Fretwell © BBC: 45, 54, 74, 101, 107, 136, 137, 153, 169, 179, 189, 207, 215, 258, 259, 267. Neil Gaiman: 12, 23 (top),33, 310 (middle left). Beth Gwinn/Michael Ochs Archive/Getty Images: 8. Ilze Kitshoff © BBC: 38, 60 (bottom right), 172, 182, 243, 244, 245, 247, 254, 255, 256, 261, 301 (middle left and bottom right), 303 (middle right), 304 (middle left), 305 (top right), 307 (bottom right), 310 (top left), (top right, bottom left and bottom right), 318, 319. Sophie Mutevelian © BBC: 2, 19, 32, 90, 96, 127, 128, 141, 156, 160, 162, 163, 164, 174, 183, 203 (top and bottom right), 210 (top and bottom left), 220, 263, 284, 287, 300 (top left), 305 (middle right), 307 (top right), 308 (bottom left), 311 (bottom left and right). The Estate of Sir Terry Pratchett: 15, 23 (bottom left and right), 25, 26, 29, 30, 31, 34, 35, 110, 170, 250, 291, 293, 294, 295, 297, 298, 301 (bottom left), 302 (middle right and bottom right), 303 (middle left), 307 (top left), 309 (bottom left), 320. Michael Ralph / Design Concept Art Illustrations © BBC: 37, 77, 88, 92, 93, 124, 145, 239, 240–1, 251, 279, 281. Steve Schofield © BBC: 104, 132, 166, 176, 204, 212, 252. Steve Schofield / Anthony Pileggi © BBC: 42, 52. Amanda Searle © BBC: 24, 178, 217, 301 (middle right).

IN THE BEGINNING

In which Terry and Neil join forces to write a novel, and enter movie development hell.

'This weather is very "*Good Omens*-y",' observes Neil Gaiman. The words that leave his lips form ghost traces in the air. He's taken refuge from the bitter London cold in a production trailer, cocooned in a coat that could double as a duvet and a hat with drop-down earflaps. The next time he makes the same observation to me, a world away from the UK in South Africa, the *Good Omens* co-author, screenwriter and showrunner has swapped the winter wear for a black T-shirt and is sheltering from a brutal sun. As he delights in pointing out, such extreme conditions are typical of the shoot and fitting for the comic fantasy odyssey about polar opposites he penned back in 1989 with the late Sir Terry Pratchett. 'It's about representatives of good and evil joining forces to prevent the coming apocalypse,' he goes on to explain. 'Which is scheduled to happen on a Saturday just after tea.'

The story behind the story is celebrated by the legion of readers who have taken the novel to their hearts. Way back in 1985 – 'pre-history' as Neil calls it – he and Terry Pratchett met in a Chinese restaurant. Terry was enjoying the early fruits of what would be huge success as the author of the Discworld series. As a young journalist, Neil had taken on a commission from a science-fiction magazine to interview the fantasy author. 'It was only a small magazine and they even asked me to take the photos,' he says. 'I was the first journalist to interview him but what I remember most is that we made each other laugh. A lot. We laughed at the same kind of things, and became friends.'

At the time, Neil had just finished writing a companion guide to *The Hitchhiker's Guide to the Galaxy* by Douglas Adams. Inspired by the unlikely combination of Adams' brand of English comic writing, Richmal Crompton's *Just William* series, about the adventures of a young schoolboy, and the

Neil Gaiman on set inside Aziraphale's bookshop, December 2017. Terry Pratchett's trademark fedora hangs on the coatrack beside him – a visual tribute to the late *Good Omens* co-author, along with a section in the shop devoted to his novels.

'We laughed at the same kind of things, and became friends.' Neil and Terry, photographed here in November 1990 at the World Fantasy Convention in Illinois.

seventies classic horror film, *The Omen*, Neil then began to form the bare bones of a story. In *William the Antichrist*, as he titled the first five thousand words before sending it to a few friends, a diabolical baby swap goes astray. Within these chapters, a laid-back demon and a prim angel decide that the Earth they have inhabited for thousands of years is too much to their liking to be destroyed. They strike a pact to shadow the Antichrist child destined to kick-start Armageddon on his eleventh birthday, unaware that the real Son of Satan is living an idyllic childhood elsewhere.

Terry Pratchett was among the select band who received the opening chapters, and there the story pauses for some time. 'My graphic novel, *Sandman*, happened,' explains Neil. 'For almost an entire year, life became about writing that. Then my phone rang. And the voice says: "That thing you sent me. I want to know what happens. Are you doing anything with it?" It was Terry. I told him I was busy, and he made me an offer. "Either sell me what you've done," he said, "or we can write it together." And because I am no fool, I told him we would write it together. Why wouldn't I? Terry knows his craft. He had fantasy tied up but nobody was writing funny horror, and here was an opportunity to write a novel with him. It was like Michelangelo asking me if I wanted to help him paint a ceiling.'

When two authors collaborate, it's often easy to see the joins. While Terry and Neil possess unique voices, *Good Omens* is a seamless read and this is testament to their talents. Since publication in 1990, readers have continued to debate how the pair created what has now become a classic. 'Anyone who assumes I did all of the dark bits and Terry did all the jokes kind of misses the point,' says Neil. 'When we wrote the book it was very simple. I had an audience of one for my bits, and he had an audience of one, which was me. The entire game for each of us was, "Can I make him laugh or wish he'd written that?" I read reviews where people assume that I had written a dark and sombre story, and Terry had stood behind me tossing out jokes like rose petals, but that's not what happened. The fact is I wrote the opening in classic English humour style, like P. G. Wodehouse, Douglas Adams and Richmal Crompton. I understood it, and so did Terry. Neither of us created it. And then Terry came in, carried on, and I carried on from there. We'd rewrite each other's pages, write footnotes for them, throw characters in and hand them over when we got stuck. Ultimately, we wrote a book together. It was all about the phone calls and the writing.'

As a measure of just how closely this process drew the strands of the story together, Neil reflects on a moment that occurred during the editing process. 'We were sitting in the damp, cold basement of Gollancz, our publisher at the time, when Terry laughed at a gag in the manuscript. "That's really good!" he said to me, but I swore that he had written it. We came to the conclusion that the manuscript had begun writing itself, which neither of us would admit to for fear of being thought weird.'

Just ahead of publication, a minor misunderstanding occurred that would launch the novel on an epic journey to the screen. Keen to share their work with people they admired, Terry and Neil sent an advance copy to Monty Python star, screenwriter and film director Terry Gilliam.

'We included a note to introduce the book,' Neil explains, 'and politely asked if he might write a quote that could be used to promote it. Only somehow the note went astray, which meant Terry Gilliam found this book on his desk with no explanation why, and just assumed it was because it might have film potential. So, he read it, and it turns out that he loved it, because the next thing we knew he was trying to buy the rights.' Neil considers his words for a moment, as he will several times throughout his account. As *Good Omens* is a novel that would take almost thirty years to reach the screen, I quickly come to realize that such a pause precedes a setback. 'Sadly, there's a fuck-up in the negotiations,' he continues finally. 'Terry Gilliam still wanted to do it, but the film rights ended up going elsewhere.'

It's here that Hollywood gets involved in the story. While the writing partnership endured under the Gaiman–Pratchett Accord, as Neil calls it, the stateside switch also marked a stint in development hell.

'It was early 1991,' says Neil. 'The book had just been published in the USA, and Terry and I were invited out to attend lots of meetings. We were put up at the Chateau Marmont on Sunset Boulevard, which was run down and seedy at the time and is now the coolest of hotels. Every morning we would write new outlines, based on the previous day's meeting and in the afternoon we would go and have another meeting with people who hadn't read the outline we'd sent to them. It was a strange experience,' he recalls diplomatically. 'Eventually, we said that we needed to go home and start writing a script, which we did. And in putting together an early draft we used characters we'd already planned to put in the sequel to *Good Omens* if ever we wrote it. So, it was there that our angels, Gabriel and Sandalphon, began life, but I also remember a lot of stuff being odd and off in that draft. Aziraphale wasn't a rare book dealer. He worked at the British Museum, and that was the location for a big scene with angels activating their halos and using them as killer Frisbees. I don't know if it was any good, but it was where a lot of the ideas started.'

It was also a point where both Terry Pratchett and Neil Gaiman saw their lives and careers take off in different directions. With their priorities elsewhere, the pair placed their film adaptation of *Good Omens* on hold. Over the two decades that followed, Terry's long-running Discworld series sold millions of copies worldwide and made him the UK's best-selling author of the 1990s. A seemingly unstoppable creative force, he described his diagnosis in 2007 of a rare form of early onset Alzheimer's as 'an embuggerance'. It saw the author publically explore what it means to live with the disease, while pledging to continue writing by any means. Meanwhile, living in the USA, Neil Gaiman wrote a string of award-winning, bestselling novels including *Stardust, American Gods* and *Coraline*. It was the animated film adaptation of the latter title that saw *Good Omens* come back into the frame – along with the man who had first hoped to take the story to the cinema.

'It was 2012, and Terry Gilliam has just hosted a screening of *12 Monkeys* in some fancy Hollywood theatre,' says Neil. 'I'm about to host a screening of *Coraline,* and so we have lunch. Way back in 1999, when the option expired on the original deal, Terry had finally managed to pick up the film rights to *Good Omens*. He'd co-written a script, raised around fifty million dollars and lined up stars such as Johnny Depp, Robin Williams and Kirsten Dunst. Terry Pratchett and I had jokingly agreed to pay him a groat if he got it made. All he had to do

was find a studio. And then 9/11 happened... So, there is Terry Gilliam pitching a movie about the end of the world, people are shaking in response and he never received his groat.' While the episode had marked yet another dead-end for *Good Omens*' movie prospects, it sparked an association between the two that would lead to a new direction for the adaptation.

'Over lunch,' Neil continues, 'Terry Gilliam says, "TV today is the new movies. I've always wanted to get a film made of *Good Omens* but I've failed. Let's do TV!" And I said, "Great."' Neil sits back in his chair as he says this, only to allow a moment to pass that's loaded with a sense of inevitability. 'This happened as he was trying to get *Don Quixote* off the ground,' he says, referring to what would come to be regarded as one of the most notoriously protracted and all-consuming movie projects in Hollywood history. 'So, Terry Gilliam dropped out of the process fairly early on. Then another Python, Terry Jones, and screenwriter Gavin Scott signed up for a draft, but Terry Pratchett and I didn't feel it hit the mark. He and I were always kind of on the same page when it came to 'the old girl' as Terry Pratchett came to call *Good Omens*, and so when the BBC acquired television rights we agreed the project had found a good home.'

Restaurants are a running theme in the story behind *Good Omens*, with Terry and Neil meeting several times over a meal to discuss plans for an adaptation. Here, the pair toast the decision to translate the story to television, having planned to make a cameo appearance in the celebrated sushi-eating scene.

With an understanding in place that they would work on the adaptation together or not at all, and with commitments keeping each of them busy, Terry and Neil opted to stand back from scriptwriting duties. 'Our line was always that we would show up and eat sushi during the sushi scene,' Neil says. 'That's all we intended to do.'

Finally, over twenty years after first publication and with fans of the book spanning generations, *Good Omens* was set to make the transition from page to screen. The stars had aligned at last, it seemed. Then Terry's health changed the course of events.

'His Alzheimer's started progressing harder and faster than either of us had expected,' says Neil, referring to a period in which Terry recognized that despite everything he could no longer write. 'We had been friends for over thirty years, and during that time he had never asked me for anything. Then, out of the blue, I received an email from him with a special request. It read: "Listen, I know how busy you are. I know you don't have time to do this, but I want you to write the script for *Good Omens*. You are the only human being on this planet who has the passion, love and understanding for the old girl that I do. You have to do this for me so that I can see it." And I thought, "OK, if you put it like that then I'll do it."

'I had adapted my own work in the past, writing scripts for *Death: The High Cost of Living* and *Sandman*, but not a lot else was seen. I'd also written two episodes of *Doctor Who*, and so I felt like I knew what I was doing. Usually, having written something once I'd rather start something new, but having a very sick co-author saying I had to do this?' Neil spreads his hands as if the answer is clear to see. 'I had to step up to the plate.'

A pause, then: 'All this took place in autumn 2014, around the time that the BBC radio adaptation of *Good Omens* was happening,' he continues, referring to the production scripted and co-directed by Dirk Maggs and starring Peter Serafinowicz and Mark Heap. 'Terry had talked me into writing the TV adaptation, and I thought OK, I have a few years. Only I didn't have a few years,' he says. 'Terry was unconscious by December and dead by March.'

He pauses again. 'His passing took all of us by surprise,' Neil remembers. 'About a week later, I started writing, and it was very sad. The moments Terry felt closest to me were the moments I would get stuck during the writing process. In the old days, when we wrote the novel, I would send him what I'd done or phone him up. And he would say, "Aahh, the problem, Grasshopper, is in the way you phrase the question," And I would reply, "Just tell me what to do!" which somehow always started a conversation. In writing the script, there were times I'd really want to talk to Terry, and also places where I'd figure something out and do something really clever, and I would want to share it with him. So, instead, I would text Terry's former personal assistant, Rob Wilkins, now his representative on Earth. It was the nearest thing I had.'

It was in these early stages that Neil formed a fierce view of how the screen version of *Good Omens* should shape up. 'While breaking down the story I felt that six hour-long episodes seemed right. There was a moment when I'd been asked to write it in a way that it could be turned into twelve thirty-minute episodes,' he adds with a wry smile, 'and I thought, "Yeah, that's never going to happen." I always knew what I wanted, and I also knew that I wanted to be showrunner. I'd written enough telly to know that it's a crapshoot for a writer.

'Take *Doctor Who*. One episode was fantastic and won lots of awards. I felt the other was a dog. And the weird thing about those two episodes was that both scripts were comparable in terms of quality. The difference was that one got shot as intended and the other one didn't because by the time we got to shooting, scenes had been randomly dropped or rewritten by the art department, who felt they couldn't deliver what had been asked in the script.'

Translating any story from one medium to another demands compromise. All manner of practical factors come into play from budget to location restrictions. In addition, what may sing on the page can fall flat visually, just as a heavy hand can see things dropped from the source material that somehow leaves the viewer feeling as if something is missing. It's a delicate process, and writers who adapt their own work also face additional challenges and possibilities. Some find themselves too close to the story to unpick it while others call upon their insight into the narrative to optimize it for the new

medium. In approaching the screenplay for a novel he had co-written as a young author, Neil Gaiman was well aware of the pitfalls, and experienced enough to steer his creative vision through the process.

'I went back to the novel all the time and picked off what I needed,' Neil explains. 'If the dialogue was good then I would steal from it. But the problem with the novel, if you listen to the audiobook version, is that it runs to twelve and a half hours. I have to point this out when people ask what has happened to their favourite dialogue. For example, there is a moment when Aziraphale and Crowley get drunk and burble about gorillas, the size of dolphin brains and *The Sound of Music*. Now, I know why this has to be three minutes and not fifteen in the adaptation, but I still miss it. There are other scenes that had to go to keep the plot moving,' he laments. 'They'll never be seen, except in my heart.'

Such decisions are always tough, but often it's the writer who sees things between the lines that will only become apparent to the audience if certain elements are left intact.

'It's easy to say, "We think this and this should go," from a production end,' Neil offers, 'and often the reason is because they're a bit expensive or

Neil on an early recce of Hambleden, the picturesque English village that would become Tadfield in *Good Omens* – and the epicentre of the coming apocalypse.

complicated. Whereas I look at it and think, "This scene here which everyone loves, actually doesn't progress the story further, and I can lose that." But all those things that you think can go, they *can't* go. They're the equivalent of having a long joke, and exciting things happen, and then you get to the punch line, and the woman holds up the talking dog, and it looks at everybody and it says, "Actually, I am Napoleon," and everyone laughs – but it's only funny if you've heard all the previous steps. And people forget that taking away the set-up no longer makes it funny or interesting. It's a dispiriting experience,' he says, 'and what occurred with *Doctor Who* was not the first time it had happened to me. So I just thought to myself that I don't want to do that again. If I'm going to spend several years of my life writing these scripts, to honour Terry's wishes, then I need to see this through.'

As Neil himself recognizes, this is an adaptation built upon the confidence that comes from three decades of writing for page and screen. But for all the wisdom of experience, he found that above all one factor guided him throughout the process. 'Terry isn't here, which leaves me as the guardian of the soul of the story,' he explains. 'It's funny because sometimes I found myself defending Terry's bits harder or more passionately than I would defend my own bits. Take Agnes Nutter,' he says, referring to what has become a key scene in the adaptation in which the seventeenth-century author of the book of prophecies foretelling the coming of the Antichrist is burned at the stake. 'It was a huge, complicated and incredibly expensive shoot, with bonfires built and primed to explode as well as huge crowds in costume. It had to feel just like an English village in the 1640s, and of course everyone asked if there was a cheap way of doing it. One suggestion was that we could tell the story using old-fashioned woodcuts and have the narrator take us through what happened, but I just thought, "No". Because I had brought aspects of the story like Crowley and the baby swap along to the mix, and Terry created Agnes Nutter. So, if I had cut out Agnes then I wouldn't be doing right by the person who gave me this job. Terry would've rolled over in his grave.'

Throughout the years since publication, and despite several valiant attempts, *Good Omens* has been famously considered by many to be unfilmable. It's a wildly inventive 400-page odyssey – complete with footnotes – that unites an angel and a demon on Earth against the forces of Heaven and Hell. 'It's a reinvention,' says Neil about his own adaptation. 'I am old enough, and have seen enough things fail, to know that we're not filming the novel. But what I can do is acknowledge that I'm making telly, and to say to people, "Yes, some of your favourite moments will probably only be in the book, but I will give you other favourite moments, and you will have some new favourite moments that didn't exist before. Is that a deal?" And that's kind of the way I approached it. It's the television draft, and I crafted it like a love story with attention to the relationship between Aziraphale and Crowley.'

With BBC Studios on board, and an awareness that an adaptation like *Good Omens* could only play out on a grand scale, Neil made a conscious decision to focus purely on telling the best story possible. 'I had to avoid asking myself how much this would cost,' he says. 'How we shot this needed to be someone else's problem. Even so, I delivered the script for Episode Six and just thought we were doomed. Why? Because I know how much television costs. There are 240 characters in the script, including aliens, in a story covering six thousand years. So I figured if they threw *Doctor Who* money at it that would be nice, but not enough.' When he talks about his ambitions for the adaptation, it's easy to wonder whether the moments of doubt Neil describes would have been softened or even avoided with his writing partner at his side. 'I became convinced that I was writing something too expensive to be made,' he says. 'There was a point, in fact, when I thought, "Why am I wasting my fucking time?"'

On delivering the scripts, Neil's concerns about costs became both a reality and an opportunity. 'The BBC responded with nothing but enthusiasm. They loved the story, but it was obviously going to be expensive. So, they went off to find a partner, which is how Amazon joined us.' As he describes the working relationship between a broadcasting institution and a pioneering force, Neil is clearly delighted by the outcome. 'We've been very fortunate,' he says. 'Take the notes that come from the studio. Often that feedback can be a challenge but with *Good Omens* it's mostly just a call or an email to say how wonderfully everything is going.' As the project gathered momentum, drawing key crew and cast, Neil notes how a spirit emerged that would go on to take them through the production process. 'It began to take on a peculiar lightning-in-a-jar quality, and I was very aware of that,' he says. 'I missed Terry, but it became a joyful experience.'

While Terry Pratchett was known for his trademark fedora (which features in the show as a touching homage, hanging on a coat stand in Aziraphale's bookshop), Neil Gaiman is a man with many hats of the metaphorical kind. He's the co-author of _Good Omens_, the novel, as well as the screenwriter and showrunner for the TV adaptation.

'It's an interesting, amorphous title,' he says of the latter. 'The showrunner in the American sense comes from the fact that often you have a lot of writers and a lot of directors coming in on a series, and so you need one person with consistency of vision. In the case of _Good Omens_, you only have one screenwriter, which is me, and you only have one director, which is Douglas Mackinnon. So, my function is less about being there for consistency of vision, and more to make sure that the thing that we're doing is the thing that's in my head.'

In practical terms, Neil considers his showrunning role to fall into two phases. 'Initially it involved working closely with Douglas and Rob on big things like casting and rehearsals,' he explains. 'I didn't really know how it was going to work. All I knew was that without me other people would be making decisions on what was going to get cut. And it can go well and it can go badly, and if you've written the script that can be the equivalent of handing over the architectural plans for a house. You give it to the builders and go away, and when you come back they say, "What do you think?" and you say, "Well, I'm not sure about the toilet." And they say, "You didn't want it purple?" and you reply, "No, I didn't really want it in the middle of the kitchen, and what about the front door?" And the builders say, "We didn't think you needed a front door." And so despite having nothing to do with the build everyone is going to ask why you designed this strange building.'

Once again, Neil cites the absence of his co-writer as his drive to ensure that _Good Omens_ translated to the screen and remained true to the original vision.

'Terry's last request to me was to make this something he would be proud of. And so that has been my job.'

Many screenwriters assemble a fantasy cast as they write the script. It can help to bring characters alive, and Neil is no exception. In the case of *Good Omens*, pursuing a vision in memory of the novel's co-writer, he set out to turn the dream into a reality.

'I had Michael Sheen and David Tennant in mind when I was writing,' he says. 'I was half way through Episode Three, scripting the scene in the church, and I suddenly decided that I wanted David. And I wrote it as if I was going to get David. It was a combination of the physicality of the character and knowing he could land every line. You write different kinds of dialogue for different kinds of actors,' he continues, 'and there's a specific kind of dialogue that you write when you know they're going to land it. You can be more playful, for example. So I hoped I'd get David when I wrote Crowley going, "Ow ow ow!" as he walked down the church aisle, and then delivering this entire speech while having to hop from foot to foot. That's not the kind of thing you'd give most actors unless you knew they were good enough to do it.'

Neil braves the cold with the two actors he had cast in his mind long before delivering the script.

In a story that explores the dynamics between opposing forces, Neil understood the importance of carefully pairing characters. With many star suggestions on the table, the *Good Omens* screenwriter and showrunner remained true to the two names that had steered him through the script.

'There is a goodness to Michael Sheen, a sweetness and a vulnerability, but also a complexity,' he says about the actor he believed could embody an angel while serving as one half of an odd couple alongside a demonic counterpart. 'In all the roles I've seen Michael play he tends to portray very hard-edged people. I just thought I would love to bring that niceness he can do into *Good Omens*.'

With every pairing in the story, there comes a point of intersection. In Neil's view, this connection is what makes his characters whole. 'There is a line in the script,' he says, 'when Aziraphale says to Crowley, "At the end of the day there is something fundamentally decent about you." And Crowley replies, "Underneath it all it's nice to know you're just enough of a bastard to be worth knowing." And that sums up why I wanted these guys. Michael could give me the complexity of an angel who also has some faults, while David's Crowley is a demon with a certain sweetness to him.'

David Tennant and the rest of the *Good Omens* cast welcomed Neil's presence on set, and regarded him as a touchstone when it came to refining their characters.

In discussing the pairing of David Tennant and Michael Sheen, Neil describes the process in which the actors sought to understand each other in their roles. 'For the first five minutes of the read-through I worried there was no chemistry,' he says. 'And then by minute ten they began to find something. By minute fifteen it was interesting, and then after lunch they were a thing. They found it somewhere in there. I just got the feeling that these two people actually like each other, enjoy acting with each other, and this is going to be good.'

Considering the moment in which David and Michael's characters locked into place with each other, Douglas Mackinnon offers one simple explanation. 'They started having fun,' he says, though adds that he was happy that it didn't happen from the first line of the script. 'Personally, I hate great read-throughs,' he says. 'It means that something's happened in that read-through that we've not filmed. My favourite read-through is a flat one where all the executives go away asking if it's going to work. Well, that's how it should work. A read-through should be dead,' he finishes, speaking as a director set to help shape the production to embody the soul of the script.

Having overseen the laying of the foundations before the shoot, from the casting to the table read-through, Neil Gaiman's role as showrunner then shifted towards a focus on detail. 'As we moved into production I tended to deal with smaller issues where departments could've got the wrong end of the stick without me,' he says. 'It means I could lean in at any time and say, "Aah, when I said we are looking at a scroll that shows the lineage of Adam, I meant it starts with the Biblical Adam going forward to Noah, rather than our Adam who is preceded by Satan."' The scroll may be a minor detail, but Neil is aware that every aspect feeds into the overall vision. It's clear that both cast and crew welcomed his input. As well as providing guidance where he felt it was needed, Neil was on hand to answer questions or provide interpretations. His presence, as he agrees, served as a touchstone for the production.

'I don't know it's something I would've done in the same way had this been my baby alone,' he admits. 'But I feel I owe it to Terry that one of us is here. Had it been only mine, I'd be more willing to go, "Well, I've written it, I've done the script, let's see what other people bring to it." Whereas with this I'm very interested in what other people bring to it, but I also want to be there.' Above all, as showrunner, Neil has sought to fit in alongside Douglas in the director's chair. 'I'm a second pair of eyes for him,' he says. 'We respect each other, and if something isn't working for me then we'll figure out how to fix it.'

Good Omens is the first time Neil has worked with Douglas, who has directed a raft of high-profile, critically acclaimed dramas and films for television. Neil points to *Jekyll*, the 2007 BBC series starring James Nesbitt, as a drama that showcased the Scotsman's talent for combining a range of narrative elements into something substantial and unique. '*Jekyll* was funny, and it was scary, and it was an adventure,' he says. 'And it meant all of those things without ever compromising any one of them or sacrificing any of those elements. I knew that in order for *Good Omens* to work we needed someone as a director who could deliver that.' Neil pauses to consider the unique nature of the story he seeks to tell. '*Good Omens* is funny, but if you don't care about the outcome, if the violence isn't violent, if the scary stuff isn't scary then it doesn't mean anything. I needed a director like Douglas who could do that, and in the past I had watched directors fail. They failed because they felt they needed one tone.'

The question of tone is one that often crops up in conversation with the cast and crew of *Good Omens*. Rather than pursuing one mood or atmosphere throughout, Neil and Douglas have created a series that weaves everything from fantastical action, philosophical reflection, bone-dry wit and creeping horror into a glorious tapestry. The result, as Neil agrees, is hard to define. 'I can't articulate it,' he says, 'but I know it when I see it. I have heard Douglas say, "Well, the Hollywood way of doing it is this, but the *Good Omens* way is that," and I understood. We're talking about something slightly out of kilter,' he suggests. 'Something beautiful but a thing of its own.'

Douglas has his own take on tone. 'It's nostalgic and zeitgeisty at the same time,' he offers, and then tables the idea that the key is in the approach to comedy. 'For me, all great writing is on the edge of absurdity,' he says. 'And in this genre we're on the edge. If you push it over the edge then it becomes stupid, whereas if we all take it seriously then somehow it works. I remember the very first auditions we had for the satanic nuns. So many were trying to do

The read-through provided the first opportunity for Neil, Douglas and executive producer, Rob, to hear the story voiced by the cast who would bring the story to the screen.

comedy accents, and then we saw Nina Sosanya. Now she's someone who loves the novel, and she did it completely straight. That was the first moment when I thought, "That thing is *Good Omens*." We see it in Michael Sheen and David Tennant as well. We have a lot of laughs on set, but not with the scripts. The comedy comes through when it's played seriously.'

Neil nods in agreement. 'We're letting the characters tell the story and not playing for laughs,' he says. 'If you care about people then it becomes funny.'

As a team, it's clear that Neil Gaiman and Douglas Mackinnon have put both heart and soul into the production. It's a wildly ambitious project that has demanded commitment as much as creativity. 'It's been really interesting doing it,' says Neil, 'and I think I'm relatively good at it, but I don't know if I would ever do this again. I can go back to being the novelist who hands his work over to the filmmaker, because there are lots of people out there who can make really good TV. It's just I don't know if there are lots of people who can write my novels. I think that's just me,' he says dryly. 'This has taken several years out of my life, but the thing is I do want to work with Douglas again. We'll have to make something else. *Good Omens* 2? Who knows?'

GOOD OMENS

ROLL	SLATE	TAKE
#A01	1	1

SCENE
1.58 PT. 1

2007

DIR: DOUGLAS MACKINNON
DOP: GAVIN FINNEY BSC

DATE: 18TH Sept '17   FILTERS: BDFx ½ IR 1.5 A

A DEAL WITH DOUGLAS

In which a Scottish director completes the unholy trinity and envisions the End of Days.

'To all fans of *Good Omens*, all I can say is that the love Terry and Neil put into the novel is followed in spades by me in this series, and by everyone else who is making it.'

With some reverence, as if it might crumble to dust, Douglas Mackinnon shows me his paperback copy of *Good Omens*. The cover is beyond tattered and struggles to contain pages bloated from being repeatedly rain soaked and sun dried. The whole thing is bristled with coloured sticky notes. It could be an ancient relic, such is the care with which the Scottish director leafs through in search of a favourite line.

'You can't wave this about and say it's unexamined,' he says. 'The detail I wanted to go into was often overwhelming.'

With Emmy award-winning television shows to his credit from *Jekyll* to *Sherlock*, *Line of Duty*, *Knightfall* and *Doctor Who*, Skye-born Douglas Mackinnon considers every step on his career path to be vital to the success of this, his most creative, bold and ambitious production to date.

'I do have a basic philosophy that your next project should be one you've been training for in your previous projects,' he offers, and goes on to stress how proud he is of everything he's worked on. 'In a way, all these huge projects became a perfect training ground for *Good Omens*. So, when I received the scripts in February 2017, I knew that I wanted to do it within the first ten to fifteen pages. By the time I'd finished reading Episode One I was messaging production saying, "I have to do this." It felt like I was just right for it, although it's for others to judge if I'm correct in that.'

In adapting *Good Omens* for television, Douglas Mackinnon is well aware that he's taking on a vastly challenging project. It's one that might have defeated

With Terry at the heart of the production, Douglas kicked off the read-through with a framed picture of the late author on his table, along with a copy of *Good Omens* and Shadwell's Thundergun should any of the cast step out of line.

many others, but then this is a director who possesses the kind of unflappable nature, unblinking gaze and ability to harness the respect and loyalty of a crew that you might expect from the captain of a supertanker. 'For me, outside family, the place I'm most at home is doing a project of this size,' he says.

Douglas is also immensely creative, with a pioneering attitude to blending live action and CGI (computer-generated imagery). 'One of my beliefs is that CGI is moving into a different phase,' he says. 'The vocabulary of television and film is now heading towards a point where it's just another storytelling tool, which is what I've tried to do in *Good Omens*. It isn't about saving the visual effects to the end because it's spectacular. We do it when it's right for the story, and from a place where it's a normal part of the world.'

Douglas goes on to mention that he first came on to Neil Gaiman's radar as a director for his work on the 2007 series *Jekyll*, written by Steven Moffatt. 'It was just before CGI came into play properly on television,' he says. 'Neil's view is that it was slightly too early or ahead of its time as we were trying techniques that seemingly weren't possible. In *Sherlock* and *Line of Duty* in particular it was about nailing performance down to tiny brushstrokes,' Douglas continues. 'Now there are lots of directors who are amazing at handling CGI and lots who are great at handling performance, but the way forward is to combine the two. I've been lucky enough to explore both areas. It's testing but hugely enjoyable.'

In reading Neil's scripts for the television adaptation of *Good Omens*, Douglas saw both technical hurdles and opportunities, as well as the chance to explore his directorial approach to the full.

'I thought that I could work my way through and make something honest, visceral, spectacular and detailed,' he says. 'It's about CGI *and* performance all in one space. Then there were the logistical challenges, which have been unlike anything I or anyone else has seen before. There are certainly lots of weird and particular things that attracted me,' he adds, 'but above all it was the enormity.'

Douglas was also drawn by the quality and complexity of storytelling in Neil's scripts, which he says reminds him of his work with *Sherlock*. 'It can be intimidating to people who read it for the first time. Initially you think you're stupid, and wonder if everyone else is getting it, but in reality these are scripts

for a modern time in that the place where they arrive is when the show is completed; when we give it lucidity.'

The pre-production phase for *Good Omens* was time-limited and intense, according to Douglas. He also believes that this short window before what would be over a hundred days of shooting worked to the advantage of the show.

'We had just two months to plan,' he says. 'All the laws of TV pre-production say that's impossible, but there is an odd contradiction here because that very pressure makes everyone creative and push very hard. It's also where the ideas start flowing, and the more involved I am here the happier I feel. So, the way I can help the two or three hundred people circling me is to make sure they understand what's coming up and to get ahead for them, and use their remarkable skills and input as fuel. They come at me with hundreds of questions every day and hundreds of emails every night, and it's my job to deal with them. The only way to get great material is for the director to be within,' he adds, and then emphasizes how important it is to go into a project of this nature with a crew that he can trust. 'We hand select everyone,' he says. 'We're building a community, and preparing to go through an awful lot in six months. So we

The table read-through allowed Neil and Douglas to refine and revise the narrative ahead of filming.

On location, Douglas worked inside a tent, which acted as a canvas cocoon. This allowed him to focus on capturing the perfect footage, courtesy of a high-definition monitor, and to filter out distractions.

have to be able to work together, go for a drink together afterwards and travel through that with a sense of humour as well as a sense of purpose.'

With the production underway in September 2017, Douglas could literally be found at the heart of it all – on location and in studio – working from inside a small black tent alongside Neil and script supervisor Jemima Thomas. From an outside point of view, this may seem like a director seeking to isolate himself. In reality, according to Douglas, it helped him to find a way to stay connected with his crew while focusing on the shoot with a hunter's eye.

'From action to cut, that's the bit that's going to be on telly. I want to be a hundred per cent absorbed in it, and the tent helps to create that environment,' Douglas says. 'My background is in stills photography, and so I'm super aware of the image quality and focus. Quite often camera operators today aren't working off eyepieces but small screens. So, I ask for two twenty-inch monitors inside the tent that are of the highest quality. I'm not precious about the screens people watch my work on, but a lot of people have fifty-inch screens in their living rooms, and that's where I have to start from. Watching it on tiny little monitors seems perverse to me.'

While the tent might help Douglas avoid distraction, he encourages crew to communicate with him where necessary. 'I want to be in touch with people, and not too far away from the floor, and I really love a zoo atmosphere in the tent, where people just dive in. I don't believe in hierarchies but I do believe in structures,' he says, 'and my job is to direct and make choices. But I also try hard not to inhibit someone from saying they can do better given the chance. So, if David Tennant comes in and says can he do one more, I think why not? It's David Tennant! The same would apply to a props guy or sound operator or anyone who shouts out. There are directors who won't listen and blank everyone out, but for me I've got to hear. So if nobody is talking to me I assume they're OK. If costume and make-up say nothing I assume they're happy. Silence means approval, and that's where the fun starts, but if anyone comes to me then I had better listen.'

Good Omens is a supersized production in every way. With well over two hundred speaking parts, a host of varied locations and six episodes to complete within a tight schedule, Douglas set a course that kept everything on track without compromise. As a director, he knows exactly what he wants, and has

Throughout filming Douglas made sure he was available to cast and crew to listen to their suggestions and work on the scenes collaboratively.

a talent for corralling cast and crew into pursuing as many takes as necessary with passion and commitment throughout.

'Directing is all about using your eyes and your ears, and saying, "That's the shot I want,"' he observes. 'I love that it's so simple, and that difficult, and it takes a long time as a director to trust in it as a concept. I've been hired for my eyes, and the tastes that people are interested in, to actually get it right. Nobody ever tells you that as a director, and you need the confidence to say, "It's me that I want as well," and then you can start.'

There is no doubt that Douglas has risen to the challenge of directing one of the most ambitious TV series in recent years. He's passionate about the story, having read the novel long ago, and delighted that its co-author and screenwriter also serves as showrunner.

'Neil fuels passion and that works in both directions,' says Douglas. 'If he comes across someone who rises up to his passion level then he will meet them with it, which is all you can ask for. I've had the privilege of working with some great showrunners and Neil is certainly one of them,' he adds. 'The ideal situation between the director and a showrunner is that they're fully

Once filming was completed, Douglas's attention turned to directing Academy-Award winning Frances McDormand's voice-over for God.

In South Africa, the heat, dust and wind created challenging filming conditions at times. While the Scottish director endured in a T-shirt, many of the crew took to covering up as best they could.

collaborating and the work is in charge. That's how it felt all the way through with Neil. We have discussions, but I can't think of a single occasion where we disagreed. If we had different opinions about anything we just shot more than one version so that when we got to the cutting room we would have a choice.'

'What's interesting is that Neil's essentially a prose writer who also writes for television and film, whereas many others are scriptwriters full stop,' he says. 'It means he's starting from a place where he thinks anything is possible. And nothing pleases me more than to surprise Neil with something we're doing, like a technique, because he's like a child in a toy store.'

There is an unrelenting creative synergy between Douglas and Neil in which both work to deliver what they refer to as 'the television draft of *Good Omens*'.

'When you're working with each other for the first time you evolve a filming vocabulary,' Douglas suggests. 'You start figuring out what each other is thinking but more importantly what the *project* wants of you. *Good Omens* wants to get made,' he says. 'It has its own energy that is way bigger than Neil or me and it comes alive in front of you. In doing so, we know what a *Good Omens* shot is. Every frame has that DNA built into it.'

Watching Douglas orchestrate a project weaving green screens into scenes with a view to creating a narrative in which live action and CGI are indivisible, it's evident that this is television at the cutting edge of creativity. In conversation, it's also clear that this is a director who is passionate about every aspect of the production. It isn't just a job, it seems, but an opportunity to steer a fantastical story that he adores from the page to the screen without compromise. Indeed, it's no coincidence that Douglas has been instrumental in assembling a cast and crew that share his enthusiasm and vision. Whether they join him as fans of the novel or converts to the script, they have united behind him in aiming to deliver a series that makes both Neil Gaiman *and* Terry Pratchett proud.

'I want this to be something people can't switch off because they feel like they might miss something,' says Douglas. 'We're not making it for the fans, but to *make* fans, and everyone should know that we love the novel down to its core. Of course, everything in the book can't be in the series, but we hope that everything people love will be in it,' he adds, and then pauses to reflect on the adaptation he has steered here. 'I want it to be joyous, and I hope that the rest of the world gets it too. That's all I can do.'

Douglas contemplates the coming of the Four Horsepersons from the comfort of his *Good Omens* director's chair.

OUTSIDE THE GATE

In which the angel, Aziraphale, and the demon, Crowley, receive unsettling news.

Fans of the novel will know exactly where they are in the opening scene. It's big, it's biblical, and the action that takes place runs from bittersweet to funny and philosophical.

Be in no doubt, *Good Omens* has begun.

Set within the Garden of Eden, at the Eastern Gate, we are introduced to the ultimate odd couple: the demon, Crowley, who has played a role in the temptation of Adam and Eve, and Aziraphale the angel, who must carry out orders and cast them out. It might take a moment to adjust your eyes to Michael Sheen's bleached white hair, and the louche darkness embodied by David Tennant. Still, their relationship of convenience quickly takes shape as they watch the shamed and exiled couple head into the wilderness armed with a flaming sword that really should have stayed in the angel's possession.

The filming schedule for *Good Omens* took place over a six-month period. Overseen with a combination of military precision and good-humoured camaraderie by Douglas Mackinnon from his director's tent, the shoot ran from mid-September 2017 to early March 2018, first across the UK followed by locations in and around Cape Town, South Africa. One look at the seemingly infinite ridges of sand under a beating sun makes it quite apparent that this opening scene wasn't filmed on a car lot in Dagenham. Nevertheless, it came as a surprise to much of the cast and crew that a desert could be found just outside Cape Town.

'The Atlantis Dunes are like a small version of the Sahara,' explains first assistant director Francesco 'Cesco' Reidy. 'I believe underneath it is a massive underground river, which is possibly how it got its name, who knows?' Discovered on a recce by Douglas, the sun-bleached sea of sand ridges proved

Ahead of filming, production designer, Michael Ralph assembled detailed location illustrations. This design for the scene of Adam and Eve's fall from grace was translated from sketch to screen in vivid detail.

an ideal backdrop to suggest that life beyond Eden was not a comfortable place to be. It was with this in mind that the production designer, Michael Ralph, began to envisage the garden itself.

'I thought that Eden should be protected,' he says. 'So we have walls sloped *outwards* at an angle. It was as much about what was being kept out as what was in it. Of course, we all know what's inside,' he adds, referring to the lush flora and fauna that the concept of Eden brings to mind, 'but what's out there really interested me. So the wall is tilted and it has spikes, and we get the sense that something horrific is beyond. Ultimately, I wanted to create the space so we can feel it,' he says of the set build that saw the wall section erected within the dunes in advance of the shoot, 'with angels on the corners protecting it.'

As Cesco points out, such an epic location for the opening scene came at a price. 'Filming in those kind of areas is difficult,' he says. 'It's exposed. It's very hot, there's no shade and you can burn easily. Bringing equipment is also a challenge,' he adds. 'Everything had to come in on a fleet of four-wheel-drive jeeps or tractor-type vehicles, and there was a huge amount to get in.'

Overseeing the operation was the producer for the South Africa shoot, Paul

Frift. 'It was challenging filmmaking,' he says. 'We put up a Bedouin tent to create shade, but once you stepped out it was like a furnace.'

Ensuring the smooth running of a shoot in such difficult conditions was just one of many challenges for Paul, who flew out to South Africa towards the end of 2017 while filming was in full swing across the UK.

Unusually for a production of this nature, but purely for availability reasons, the role of producer was split between himself and Phil Collinson, who covered the British leg that preceded it. 'It was tough,' says Paul. 'You have a machine that's up and running, and it's a big machine. I felt a bit like I was taking the baton in a relay.' With this in mind, and the smooth running of the shoot to ensure on location and in a Cape Town studio, Paul began planning long in advance. 'We knew we'd be filming there from the start,' he says. 'So in December I began work with a service production company and set up an office in the city. We appointed a location manager and assembled a local crew to support those coming over from the UK shoot. It meant my job was to take that, make it work and get the best out of them.'

As for the decision to stage some of the shoot in South Africa, Paul alludes to creative opportunities as much as budgetary savings. 'We're able to show places much more convincingly here that we just can't do in the UK,' he says, referring not just to the opening scene in the desert but locations and backdrops for an African village, the archaeological remains of a Middle Eastern city and a Californian condo, as well as sites for the recreation of the Crucifixion and Noah's Ark. 'The other side of the coin is that in theory you get more bang for your buck,' he adds. 'You can go for scale and have more extras. You even have more animals for your money,' he says with a smile.

With the opening scene's beyond-the-wall material in the can, the next step involved finding a suitable Garden of Eden. On paper, filming in a sub-tropical part of the world, Cape Town offered a wealth of location rich in exotic plants and foliage. In reality, production took place during one of the region's worst droughts in recent history with accute water shortages. Cesco Reidy explains that the prospect of staging a Garden of Eden scene complete with a lush waterfall became potentially problematic.

On location at Atlantis Dunes outside Cape Town, the *Good Omens* cast and crew worked under a searing sun to complete the Garden of Eden scene – featuring the first of production designer Michael Ralph's circular motifs, which run throughout the series.

'We had settled on a place called the Cascade Country Manor,' he says. 'It's a beautiful building, which was built by the Duke of Bedford just after the Second World War in an area called Paarl. This particular location has the most magnificent waterfall spilling over a rocky cliff.' The plunging water would provide the ideal backdrop as Adam and Eve fell from grace, but it needed to be plentiful for maximum visual impact. 'Of course our immediate question was would there be any water in a drought?' Cesco continues. 'So we had to ask the special effects department to find a way to pick up water from the bottom and redistribute it to the top. It was a complicated business, but much to our surprise we found there was still some water coming down, which really helped. Despite the problems in the city, this water was sourced from the mountains, so we were able to make it work.' With the addition of an apple tree, the central feature of Michael Ralph's beautiful and intricate set design, *Good Omens* begins in a manner that leaves viewers prepared for a treat.

What's more, when Adam and Eve are cast from Paradise through a hole in the wall, so *Good Omens* commences a visual preoccupation with circles that will come to be invested with meaning as the story unfolds...

Over the dunes and far away. The South African scenery enabled Douglas to represent the enormity of the world that awaits Adam and Eve outside the gates.

AZIRAPHALE

MICHAEL SHEEN

'This is me being able to do my part to bring to the screen a book I've always loved.'

True to the spirit of *Good Omens*, Michael Sheen's introduction to the novel is in complete contrast to that of his co-star.

'I read the book when it first came out,' says the Welsh-born stage and screen actor, acclaimed for his Hollywood movies as much as his in-depth portrayal of roles as diverse as Tony Blair, Brian Clough and Kenneth Williams. 'I was in my first year at drama school, fresh in London and open to new ideas and influences, when a friend introduced me to Neil's work. Around this time comics were having a new kind of life, respect and fan base. They weren't based on superheroes any more, and you had people like Neil Gaiman and Grant Morrison and Alan Moore coming through. So this friend gave me titles like *Sandman*, *Watchmen*, *V for Vendetta* and *Swamp Thing*. I read them and I loved them, but Neil's *Sandman* was the one I loved the most. Then I saw there was a book out he had written with Terry, whose work I didn't know at that point. And so I got it and I read it and I thought it was fantastic. Subsequently, I got my hands on everything that Neil had written and started reading Terry's books as well. But it was Neil I stuck with and enjoyed and that opened up all other kinds of avenues in science fiction and fantasy.'

One such avenue, as Michael explains, led to an approach from the *Good Omens* co-author himself.

'Years down the line,' he says, having appeared in Hollywood blockbusters such as *The Twilight Saga: New Moon*, *Underworld: Rise of the Lycans* and *Tron: Legacy*, 'people were asking me during interviews why an actor who had appeared in *The Queen* and *The Special Relationship* was drawn to genre films. So in my defence of fantasy and science fiction I talked about my favourite writers, such as Philip K. Dick, Stephen King and Neil Gaiman. Then one day there was a knock at my door, and I took delivery of a large box. I opened the box and in it was a card from Neil. He'd read one of my interviews. And the card said, "From one fan to another", and in the box were all these wonderful books of his, including special editions. So the next time he was near where I lived we met up, and we've been friends ever since.'

With Michael Sheen and Neil Gaiman in the same orbit, it was perhaps inevitable that two creative talents in their respective fields would consider working with one another.

'Neil talked about the different attempts to make *Good Omens*, and I was around when some of it was happening. Eventually, after Neil had written the script himself he sent it to me. I was happy to do anything he had done, so there was no question about it. If they wanted me then I was on board, no matter what. As time went on, it became clear that I would be best suited to Aziraphale, and that seemed to make sense. It's a fantastic cast, and you can't imagine anybody playing anyone else.'

When I ask him to expand on his character, Michael Sheen immediately frames Aziraphale in terms of the angel's relationship with Crowley. 'They're both unique and special in their own ways,' he says, referencing their role as forces for good and evil, 'but the edges get knocked off them a little bit the longer they are on Earth and interacting with human life. So, instead of being black and white everything becomes a little bit greyer.' Here, Michael points out that both Aziraphale and Crowley take things further into unknown territory by abandoning their positions as polar opposites and effectively joining forces.

'I use the analogy of the Beatles,' he says. 'When the four were first becoming huge, this phenomenon, nobody could understand what they were going through. And it was because nobody else had ever gone through that kind of fame or adulation before that it bound them together. I think there is something similar between Crowley and Aziraphale. Nobody else can understand what it's like to be on Earth among humans as they have been, and so there's a bond that comes out of that. And as that connection grows over time it starts to mean they have more in common with each other than they do with their "own kind". They become a slightly separate team.'

With Michael Sheen on board at an early stage, costume designer Claire Anderson worked closely with the actor in dressing Aziraphale – as seen here in sketches ahead of a fitting session.

As well as coming to *Good Omens* in contrasting ways, Michael Sheen and David Tennant have also approached their roles very differently.

'They're both incredibly deep as actors,' observes Neil Gaiman. 'David comes in with an idea of what he wants to do, he'll make a stab at it and if we want something different we'll tell him. Michael is all about technique,' he continues. 'He wants to talk about it and work it through. So, there's a difference in how they pitch and play it.' On screen, the result is a unique chemistry between an angel and a demon that makes them a memorable double act.

'There is no Crowley without Aziraphale,' says Michael, 'and there is no Aziraphale without Crowley. Of all the things I've done, I thought less about who my character is here and more about how he relates to that character.'

As for his own take on approaching a role for stage or screen, Michael ventures that everything begins with the script. With *Good Omens*, however, that starting point was the novel itself. 'One of the most important things in the process of playing anything is that first contact with the story and the character,' he says. 'The way it impresses on you and the feelings it gives you is what propels you through the whole thing. In this instance there was the book,

ABOVE: A saintly and familiar-looking gardener educates Warlock in the importance of having love and reverence for all living things.
OPPOSITE: Aziraphale as we first see him – in his Heavenly robes waiting for the VFX team to add flames to his sword.

and so I looked for clues left by Neil and Terry. Just little specific things, such as how a character is described in a certain way.'

Michael was particularly interested in the fact that Neil Gaiman adapted the work so many years after co-writing the novel. 'I felt he came back as a much more mature writer,' he says. 'The voice of the novel is certainly influenced by Douglas Adams, as Neil was at the time, and although the script still has that element you can see how he comes through it bringing different qualities.'

Michael talks about how some scripts can be restrictive by providing too much information, while others fall short. In this case, having formed the platform he needed, the actor points to collaboration as the means of investing his character with body and soul.

'I had conversations with Neil and Douglas about the story and the character, and so it starts to develop a little bit. Some things Neil would have a definite opinion on, and then there were others where he didn't want to be too prescriptive because he wanted me to bring what I thought to it as well. Then I had conversations with the costume designer, Claire Anderson, and she brings her character sketches and we start to collaborate, and the same

A man at peace. With his bookshop closed for the night, Aziraphale settles back in his chair with a glass of wine in hand and Schubert's String Quintet on the gramophone.

process occurs about hair and make-up. We're talking about the look of the character here, and still playing around with ideas, and then suddenly I'm sitting there next to David at the table read-through and you have to just open your mouth. That's when you get a feel for who this person really is,' Michael explains. 'You also have a gut response to the character beside you. So, my version of Aziraphale starts to get a bit more flesh on his bones in response to what David is doing. But until I actually stand there in costume, next to him, on set, and they say "Action", I'm never really sure what's going to come out. And then I have to let go,' he says. 'All that stuff I've just described, all those conversations, the costume fittings and readings, the drawings of what my bookshop will look like, the pictures, ideas and feelings – those will turn into something and as an actor you just let that happen.'

One of the most striking aspects of Michael Sheen's Aziraphale is the physicality of his character. Visually, the bleached blond hair and penchant for Victorian-era clothing is at the forefront, but then Michael can convey anything from humour to alarm from the lifting of an eyebrow at just the right moment. 'It's not conscious,' he insists. 'What tends to happen is that I get an instinctive response to the character and the tone of the piece, but I don't think too much about how that will express itself in the performance.' In considering where the comedy might come from, Michael takes a holistic view.

'Expressing who this person is, what he wants, what he loves, what he's scared of and those sort of things is done in all kinds of ways,' he ventures, 'and an important one is the physicality. Now, if that's funny then great. Something intrinsically interesting about Aziraphale is that he's quite fussy. He enjoys the life of humans, the finer things, and so putting him into situations where things are a bit off kilter I find amusing. It's always interesting to watch characters in uncomfortable situations, as fish out of water,' he continues. 'The action film version of that is seeing a character in danger all the time. In drama it's conflict and in comedy it's people in embarrassing or awkward situations.'

Michael Sheen is an actor who clearly enjoys bringing together the complexity of a character, rather than foregrounding one element and playing it for laughter or tears. 'For me, it's about keeping a rich and imaginative world going

AZIRAPHALE: But I won't fail. I mean, that would be bad. If I did.

Reporting for duty. Aziraphale updates his archangel colleagues on his activities at the Dowling residence.

AZIRAPHALE: Well then. Welcome to the End Times.

on in your head while you're in that character, and keeping that alive and vivid. It's about being responsive to that, and not thinking too much about how it's coming across. So the story gets expressed through the character and the character expresses itself through me.'

Even as he approaches the end of an intensive filming schedule, one that has taken him from UK airfields in the grip of winter to sun-baked South African sand dunes, Michael is still brimming with enthusiasm.

'It's been a dream job,' he says. 'I've been able to do my part to bring to the screen a book that I've always loved. Neil is one of my favourite writers, and I'm playing a character I really love, opposite someone who I think is brilliant, doing fantastic work. Then there's Douglas, who has brought enthusiasm, a sense of humour, and a real openness to the process. I also get to dress up in great outfits,' he points out. 'It's like dressing up when you're a kid, and the reason why I wanted to be an actor in the first place is because I enjoy all that.

'But more than anything else I've done,' he adds, 'this has been so dependent on what David is doing. When I look back I'll only ever be able to think about what I did in it by thinking about what David did.'

Through the centuries Aziraphale and Crowley have come to a mutual understanding that means that as Armageddon approaches they can be found comparing notes over a late-night drink.

CROWLEY

DAVID TENNANT

'I forget about the hair.
As I'm Scottish I think there's a bit of red
in there anyway. I'm very used to it now.'

 Sporting locks that could blend with a pillar-box is a guaranteed way for someone to turn heads. David Tennant is used to attention, given his starring roles in *Broadchurch* and, of course, *Doctor Who*. Having committed to the look by dyeing his hair from day one of the shoot, however, he seems surprised when I mention it. It's also a reflection of just how naturally he has taken to the figure whom Terry Pratchett and Neil Gaiman describe in the novel as 'An Angel who did not so much Fall as Saunter Vaguely Downwards'.

'Crowley is just a fantastic character in an extraordinary, mind-bending story,' he says when asked what drew him to the production. 'There's nothing else really like that out there. It's incredibly ambitious. It needs enormous resources, time and care, and as that's all available then it's something I want to be part of. This particular world that Neil and Terry created is so unique and fantastical, and yet so recognizable,' he stresses. 'It's the very domesticity of these supernatural beings that makes them so appealing to play.'

With dark glasses hiding his serpentine eyes, a rake-thin appearance and displaying a sharp sense of fashion throughout the ages, David Tennant's Crowley comes across as a fully formed demon on Earth in his own right. From the moment we meet him as he slithers up to Aziraphale in the Garden of Eden, it's clear that this embodiment of evil is mischievous, inventive and highly entertaining. Alongside Aziraphale, dressed in white from head to toe and played by Michael Sheen as a force for good, it becomes clear that these two halves form more than the sum of their parts.

Dark colours and sharp, striking lines informed Crowley's costume, while David considered his hair styles through the ages as a means of marking the passage of time.

'They complete one another,' agrees David. 'They're the perfect yin and yang. Over thousands of years on Earth, they've slightly dabbled in each other's territory, and they've been diluted by the world of men. So, Crowley has drawn Aziraphale into the odd temptation and yet Crowley isn't nearly as bad as he might be.'

For representatives of good and evil, it's the middle ground where Crowley and his counterpart come alive. In some ways, either despite God's ineffable plan or because of it, circumstance has compelled the pair to join forces. Together, they're not on the side of good or evil, but 'our side', as the angel tells the demon.

'In very strict terms it means they've been cut off by their head offices,' explains David. 'They're no longer towing the party line. Therefore, they are on their own. They have no higher power to appeal to, no authority to get them out of trouble, because they've gone too far against what is expected and prescribed. That's what "our side" means,' he says. 'I suppose they've found this way of being through the centuries where they've helped each other out a bit. They've come to realize that if one is going to cancel out the other's deeds then what is the point? I suppose the argument is that there's an equilibrium there to keep the world going round, and that you need a bit of both.' David pauses for a moment. 'I think if Terry and Neil have a philosophy here it's that extremism of any kind is unpalatable.'

David Tennant's observation reflects the fact that both the novel and the adaptation are effectively positioned in the eye of a fantastical storm. It's a tale that explores uncompromising forces at odds with one another, but does so with great heart from the centre ground. From a storytelling point of view, David believes this also has an advantage. 'It's where we create characters we grow to love,' he says. 'It's like we love the maverick cop who gets things done by not going against the rules but teasing them slightly. Their superintendent is usually the grumpy, by-the-book character we're not encouraged to find appealing. I think as human beings it's inevitable that we're melting-pot shades of grey. The supposed extremities of Heaven and Hell just seem a bit implausible.'

Following unholy orders. Crowley prepares to switch the Antichrist-in-a-basket for a newborn baby on Earth, and set the clock ticking for Armageddon.

In bringing the forces of good and evil to a point where they meet, David Tennant and Michael Sheen became aware that boundaries began to blur not just as characters but as actors. 'We often joked with each other that if we were doing this in theatre then we'd be alternating roles,' says David. 'It does cry out for it, really. Crowley and Aziraphale have found each other in this eternal commission that they're working on. They are very different, of course, but I'm sure Michael and I could've had a go. The characters themselves are significantly different but require a similar sort of actor, and that's quite nice. I've known Michael for years, and we've done similar parts in that time, which means he's the kind of actor I never get to work with. That's why this structure works for us,' he says of *Good Omens*. 'We get to do so much together.'

Existing in the novel for nearly three decades, Crowley is a character that many readers will recognize in their minds. Coming to *Good Omens* without having read the book, David admits to some initial trepidation. 'I don't know how I managed to avoid it,' he says jokingly. 'For so many people, this is such an important world. They love it, and they're really excited about it being made, and possibly true devotees might be a little nervous as well,' he adds. 'Because if you love

Go to sleep and dream of pain. Crowley keeps a close eye on a potentially diabolic child.

something that much it's very precious to you. To think that a number of people might be traipsing through car parks making a film of it might be unsettling.'

It's clear that David feels some weight of expectation from the novel's fans. He's also wise enough as an actor to know how to deal with it. 'You just have to be true to the character,' he says. 'Like with a great play, the first thing you have to do is abandon the fact that Laurence Oliver once played the same role. That baggage is never helpful.'

Having worked together on several episodes of *Doctor Who*, David talks about Douglas Mackinnon's presence at the helm as another source of confidence and reassurance. 'Douglas knows the book backwards,' he says of the director. 'He knows the script, understands what impact each scene has from one episode to the next, and protects that very wisely and astutely.'

Fresh to the book and the script, but confident in the production, how did David find his own definition of the demon?

'It's hard to unpick how you end up doing something,' he admits. 'You read the script and register it, and then it filters through your subconscious, and finally something comes out the other end. Sometimes you get confused about what's instinct and what's calculation,' he adds. 'It's not always easy to specify how things emerge. You almost don't want to go too deeply into it. Either it feels right or it doesn't, and that's a combination of many things: your initial reaction to the script, the conversations you then have with those creating it... and that includes people from all sides of the production. They might come with ideas that never occurred to you. That sets off a chain of events, and something can end up miles away from where it started.'

As an example, David goes on to explain how initial conversations with *Good Omens*' costume designer Claire Anderson, along with hair and make-up designer Anne 'Nosh' Oldham, as well as his own hair and make-up artist, Stevie Smith, played a key role in the visual creation of Crowley.

'They had the notion of long red hair,' he says. 'It wasn't in the book, but red seemed quite appealing as he's from the flames. There's also a part of me as an actor who likes to transform. So we talked about whether having it long might make him look like a rocker, rather than of the moment. Eventually we settled on

a nice, short funky red cut. Then we see him moving through time with different lengths and styles. When I was reading through the script, just plotting through what happens when was quite tricky, and so it works as a marker. And I felt that Crowley would do that in a way that perhaps Aziraphale wouldn't as he's more steady through the centuries. So that shows how a conversation about appearance sparks a few ideas that feed back into the character, and you end up dyeing your hair red for five months! Still, it meant I wasn't wearing a wig every day, and all credit to Neil who has lived with this but was still able to say, "Yeah, long red hair! That's a great idea!"'

David acknowledges that Neil Gaiman's presence on set in his role as showrunner has been a virtue throughout the production. 'Neil is the ultimate arbiter, but also very interested in what people bring,' he says. 'It's quite rare that the author of the source material would then adapt it and take charge as showrunner. It could've been quite limiting, especially because Neil is conscious that he's carrying Terry Pratchett on this journey, and that's deeply important to him. If he was a more insecure writer he might be more inclined to say: "No, it says on the page that he's wearing this, does things this way." Instead, if

Fantastically evil. Crowley reports to his fellow demons on the progress of his schooling of the Antichrist.

Inside Crowley's apartment is a safe hidden behind an early version of the Mona Lisa and a throne fit for a demon. The safe is home to a tartan flask of Holy Water, which needs handling with care.

CROWLEY: This is ridiculous. You are ridiculous. I don't even know why I'm still talking to you.

someone has a reflection on a character he's known all these years, he's interested in how they see it.

'Neil's presence is essential in terms of knowing we're being true to what's been written,' continues David, 'and yet he's gracious enough to appreciate that you might find something truer by not necessarily following it. I admit I was nervous that a writer of his status would have every right to tell us how to do it. Instead, because he's so creative and inspired by the world around him, Neil is interested in this being something we're making *together*. It's been incredibly inspiring,' he says. 'Every couple of days there's been some new extraordinary place or circumstance or special effect to work with. So, I feel like we're creating something that I believe in. Even if people don't see what they're necessarily expecting I trust they will be caught up in the world we're creating. It might not be exactly the same as what they imagine, but it will be equally pleasing. The challenge is being clever, creative and mischievous enough for the material. And we do have the boss here,' he adds with a smile. 'We've been endorsed by the authors, so can't go too far wrong.'

St James's Park is the location for many of Crowley and Aziraphale's clandestine, and rather fraught, encounters.

NUNS 'N' GUNS

In which a demonic baby switch goes hellishly wrong, and we discover that paintballing really packs a punch.

'It shone like a diamond,' says location manager Nick Marshall on describing the moment he discovered the Buckinghamshire park and mansion that would be transformed into a convent and later a corporate events facility. 'It was empty, and so it became our playground.'

There's one born every minute, so they say, unless you're the Son of Satan – in which case you arrive on Earth in a basket courtesy of two Dukes of Hell. It falls to Crowley to switch the satanic baby with a newborn, and then shadow the unsuspecting parents as they raise the boy who will trigger Armageddon on turning eleven. And so we find him lurking outside St Beryl's, a former convent turned birthing hospital, preparing to swap the child with the mewling offspring of the American ambassador and his wife, Tad and Harriet Dowling. There's another couple with a bundle of joy in the next room, the lovely and unassuming Deirdre and Arthur Young, but this is a straightforward exchange. What could possibly go wrong?

While Crowley's plan might have slipped up, triggering the start of the story, the *Good Omens* crew undertook the convent shoot with necessary precision. Occurring very early in the schedule, it also gave them a taste of what was in store.

'We were just finding our feet, and this was a complex shoot with real babies in blankets and other challenges,' says script supervisor Jemima Thomas. 'It was when we started to realize how epic in nature this shoot was going to be.'

Bulstrode Park stands just outside Gerrards Cross in Buckinghamshire, north-west of London. It's an imposing, Grade-II listed building with rooftop spires and mature gardens. Once production designer Michael Ralph had finished with both the interior and exterior, the cast and crew began work in an environment shot through with sinister undertones.

The devil in the details. From the inverted cross to the statue of a conquering serpent, the less-than-welcoming St Beryl's Hospital contains a host of hidden meaning courtesy of production designer Michael Ralph.

Every aspect of the birthing hospital at St Beryl's is welcoming to expectant parents but just a little... off.

'The monasterial side was great to embrace,' says Michael, referring to what would be home to the Chattering Order of nuns who run the hospital and fulfil their destiny by assisting Crowley in switching the babies. 'Through the main doors, I wanted to place something inside that the camera cannot ignore but has to explore. Now, there is a famous statue of a snake being killed by a Herculean character,' Michael continues with a hint of glee. 'I wanted one like it but the other way round, so ours depicts the Herculean character being killed by the *snake*. Then we had this idea that whenever you look away you hear it move, and when you look back there's a little bit of sandstone on the floor where the snake has slightly shifted.'

With special effects supremo Danny Hargreaves and his team hard at work conjuring thunder and lightning to accompany the arrival of Crowley and his precious cargo, the sequence is rich in atmosphere, fast moving and dramatic. It was also vital that the crew got everything in the can on schedule so the location could be re-dressed in a different guise altogether.

'The building had to be seen from two different periods in history, separated by eleven years,' first assistant director Cesco Reidy explains. 'The baby switch

Sinister service. Cast and crew congregate outside Bulstrode Park, in its guise as St Beryl's, to film a late-night exchange between Crowley and the Dukes of Hell.

takes place at the beginning of that period, and then later on in our story Aziraphale and Crowley pay a visit as they try to figure out what's happened to the Antichrist. By then, the convent has become Tadfield Manor, a club for corporate events. So we had to develop a schedule that allowed us to move around the building, getting the stuff set in the earlier days, while behind us and sometimes ahead of us the production and design department were changing or preparing the sets. It was challenging,' he admits. 'We were still getting to know one another, after all, but that familiarity can only come by going through difficulties and finding solutions together. It actually strengthened our camaraderie and our bonding as a unit.'

Eleven years later, on his return to the scene of the diabolical switcheroo, this time with Aziraphale in tow, Crowley finds himself in a very different setting. Gone are the the Satanic Nuns of the Chattering Order of St Beryl's and their movements in the shadows. Now, with St Beryl's never having risen from the ashes, they find the building transformed. Instead, the demon and his angelic associate walk into Tadfield Manor, which has been converted into a venue for office teambuilding away days. Across the manor grounds, an

Harriet Dowling (Jill Winternitz) is rushed into the St Beryl's labour ward in a fast-moving scene that sets the pace early in the *Good Omens* story.

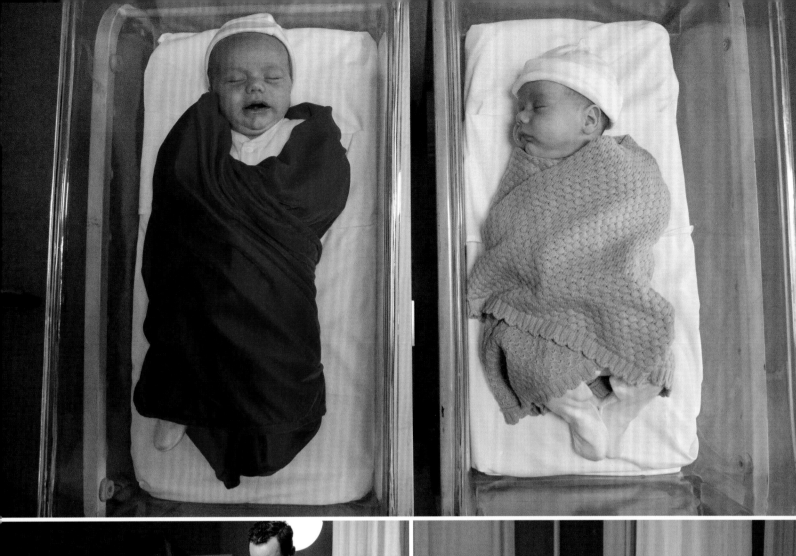

Two acting tots make their first screen appearances as part of the demonic baby-switch sequence overseen by Sister Mary Loquacious on unsuspecting parents, Mr and Mrs Young.

interdepartmental paintball skirmish is in full swing. Naturally, in the presence of such entities, the exercise becomes something altogether more dangerous and deadly.

'Michael Ralph did a fantastic job of transforming the forecourt outside the building by dressing it as a battle zone,' says Cesco. 'We had military vehicles, camouflage nets and an obstacle course. It really was fit for purpose as an adventure playground for grown-ups with guns.'

In order to make the most of the conflict and the chaos that ensues, Douglas Mackinnon and the director of photography, Gavin Finney, called in the high-speed Phantom camera.

'You see it used on football replays, shooting a ridiculous number of frames per second,' explains script supervisor Jemima Thomas. 'We wanted to see the paintballs flying as Crowley and Aziraphale walk through in super slow mo, and we staged and choreographed it carefully so they didn't get splattered.'

While the pair depart without a mark on them, leaving bedlam in their wake, there's no escaping the enormity of the task they face. For the Antichrist is missing, and Armageddon a matter of days away.

Eleven years after the swap, reeling from the discovery that he botched it, Crowley returns to the scene with Aziraphale in tow and finds St Beryl's transformed into something rather different.

The former birthing hospital is transformed into the kind of corporate training centre where middle managers can become paintball warriors for a day.

TADFIELD MANOR

CONFERENCE AND MANAGEMENT TRAINING CENTRE

A PLACE TO INTERGRATE AND EXPAND

United Worldwide Holdings (Holdings)

COMBAT INITIATIVE COURSE

SISTER MARY LOQUACIOUS / MARY HODGES

NINA SOSANYA

'Good Omens has just been one of my go-to books that I read over and over. I also have a terrible memory. I get to the end of a novel and can't remember any of it, which means I have a great time!'

Nina Sosanya makes no effort to hide her joy in being a part of the production. She's naturally funny and self-depreciating, and in her element here. Playing the satanic nurse with a heart, Sister Mary Loquacious, and her later incarnation as Tadfield Manor events host, Mary Hodges, Nina freely admits to being a long-time disciple of the novel. 'I always felt like only I knew about the book,' she says, on revealing that she reads *Good Omens* as frequently as once a year. 'I had no idea how popular it was, and then I got a call from my agent about the audition. I went so silent she thought that the line had gone dead. I began wracking my brain for any character that I could be in it. Then she said, "I don't know how you'll feel about this, Nina, but it's for a satanic nun–' and I replied: "Yes, yes... Sister Mary Loquacious. I know. OK!"'

As someone so familiar with the story, how did Nina respond to the script? 'It's a celebration of the book, it had exactly the same spirit, and Neil has adapted it brilliantly because you can't tell it in the same way as you can in a novel. But the humour of it is exactly there, and the weight of it as well. It's really funny, but like all good sci-fi and fantasy it has really interesting themes and morals.'

In the same way that Crowley and Aziraphale blur the boundaries of good and evil, Sister Mary Loquacious also occupies a curious no man's land of values.

'She's not all bad for a Satanist,' chuckles Nina. 'She's just been born into a family who worship the devil. But only in the same way that you or I might do

SISTER MARY: Fancy me holding the Antichrist. And counting his little toesy-wosies...

Sister Mary Loquacious and Crowley prepare to stage the satanic baby switcheroo.

macramé. It's just part of her family life, her upbringing, but that doesn't mean she's much different to anyone else. She's actually a rather lovely lady and the institution bit really suits her personality. She loves the Chattering Order. In the novel she's described as naturally chatty, but even though she could be a clever, bright individual, she's just found it easier to be part of St Beryl's where everyone gets on. She's also a nurse, which is useful. It's just she has a pointy wimple and an upside down cross.'

Visually, the costume designer, Claire Anderson, had to design an outfit for Nina and her fellow sisters of the Chattering Order that conveyed their beliefs with subtlety. In essence, Mary Loquacious, Grace Voluble and Teresa Garrulous needed to look recognizable as traditional sisters but with a sinister undertone.

'We looked at nuns over time in search of the most satanic,' Claire explains, and describes images she sourced of sisters sporting imposing, hooded headwear. 'In the end we felt that pointy hats symbolized something more witch-like and devilish,' she continues. 'We didn't want the viewer to see evil in the face. It was just there if they wanted it, with repeat exposure to the nuns, slowly becoming more apparent.'

The infernal infant exchange also involves the hand of Sister Teresa Garrulous (Maggie Service).

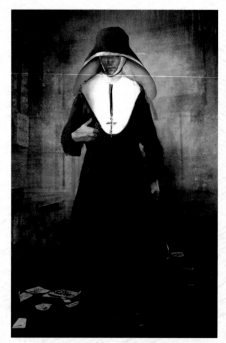

Claire considered a range of headwear for the nuns, but ultimately the hoods and shrouds were overshadowed by the witch-like hats, and then accessorised their uniforms with fiendish fob watches.

'I'd never have envisioned the pointy habit thing,' admits Nina. 'But I thought it was so well imagined, and also the fact that our habits were off the floor so you could see our feet. When we were all together we looked like this bizarre forest of black Christmas trees. There was something rather wonderful about it as we got this instant sisterhood. You can identify your club. That's the power of a uniform,' she observes. 'All we could really see of ourselves was our funny faces, with no make-up on and additional warts and facial hair.' Nina Sosanya is clearly thrilled at playing Sister Mary, and then dressing down in her post-nun reinvention as Mary Hodges. 'It was joyous for me,' she says, 'and so the challenge was in wanting to do it justice, for Terry and for Neil, and the Terry that Neil carries in his head, and for my favourite book.' When pressed for a high point from the experience, she responds not so much as an actress who nails both incarnations but as a genuine and heartfelt fan.

'My copy of *Good Omens* is a falling-apart paperback edition that looks like a Cornish pasty,' she says, and I wonder if it might even upstage Douglas's copy. 'I've had it all my life. Only now it's signed by Neil himself, which is pretty astonishing, really!'

We meet again. Nearly eleven years later, Sister Mary has reinvented herself as Mary Hodges, a woman in charge of Tadfield Manor where dust-ups between a demon and an angel will not be tolerated.

A. Z. FELL AND CO.

In which a London bookshop does little business, and the missing Antichrist child causes Crowley and Aziraphale great concern.

'What I love about Michael's sets is that they're made for the camera. You never get a sense that they're huge or cluttered. Everything is there for a reason.'

Like every member of the cast and crew, Neil Gaiman talks about the work of the production designer, Michael Ralph, with an air of respect and some awe. On *Good Omens*, this ranges from sets depicting everything from the pinnacle of Heaven to the depths of Hell. But perhaps the most striking build of all is for a location squarely on Earth. In Soho, London, to be precise.

'Aziraphale's bookshop is a massive part of the show,' says the UK producer, Phil Collinson – in fact it's the only set to appear in every episode. But this was no real-life location appropriated for the shoot. The store, as well as several streets, were carefully constructed by Michael Ralph and his team at Bovingdon Airfield in Hertfordshire, north-west of London. 'It would've been easy to go to a real bookshop,' Phil continues, 'but what Douglas managed to do here is get a sense of Soho and then give us scale and shots you wouldn't otherwise see. We were able to do things with cranes and drones that we just couldn't have done in Soho for real, and so there's a real "wow" factor.'

'It was amazing,' agrees script supervisor Jemima Thomas. 'The whole thing about Aziraphale's bookshop is that everything is beautiful and valuable and has some kind of value, whether it's monetary, antique or its precious nature. Then, when you went out of the bookshop it looked like a real street with hundreds of people and cars.'

In terms of scale alone, the Soho build was an impressive sight, and yet Michael Ralph is clear that every aspect existed purely to be seen through the camera lens.

Michael Ralph's stunning vision for Aziraphale's bookshop, rich in circular motifs, was closely translated into the finished set design.

'My role is to overview the design and the look of the production,' begins the charismatic and deep-thinking Australian-born production designer. 'It's almost an invisible middle ground that has to do with sound, lighting and camera psychology. I influence it so completely that my aim is to seduce everyone from Douglas to Gavin Finney so they see things in a certain way. They're very good at what they do, and will see the best shots I've enabled, so mine is an invisible manipulation.'

As director of photography, Gavin Finney relishes Michael's work. 'Michael is brilliant,' he says. 'He's a creative genius who rejoices in giving me things to play with. He loves moving through space, so he designs sets you don't just admire from one angle. They keep working as you go through, and have texture and layers. He's also a designer who understands light, just as Douglas does.'

Beginning with the script, the esteemed production designer explains how he approaches his work.

'I have an immense faith in my original sense of how things should look,' says Michael. 'It's the fingerprint, and I stay true to it throughout. Like an architect, you don't know where the first line starts. But if you have a strength

The bookshop exterior sits upon the corner of a crossroads – traditionally sites for hangings and the burial of witches.

Michael Ralph's design was realised in minute detail by the props team, complete with vintage cash registers, carefully sourced furniture and thousands of books.

of commitment to an original idea, and you can communicate that to people convincingly by concept then that is *everything*. People are drawn into it. They can see the show immediately and it becomes real. If I've depicted that for them then they can't see it any other way. It's such a massage of their imagination, from the colour to the toning, that they want it to be like that. With that commitment,' Michael continues, 'I have a licence to grow it organically and thread every aspect of that set into the fabric of the story.'

Such is his care and attention to the set build that Michael originates everything he can. 'There is a familiarity to the things you find in hire shops and prop stores,' he says. 'So, I buy furniture or build stuff to make it look handmade, original or priceless. I'm big on broad strokes, but also what's contained within those strokes. I understand levels and the depth of what the camera can pick up.'

Michael Ralph has an eye for detail that may not be immediately apparent to the viewer as so much of it is communicating on a subliminal level. He talks at length about how an accumulation of small things on screen can convey meaning that transcends the human eye.

'Take the bookshop,' he says by way of example. 'I located it on a corner with four streets, because as Aziraphale is an angel and came from that far back then he'd be tied to the history of the crossroads. Everything from speeches to hangings happened there. What's more, those four streets are meaningful when you consider the Four Horsepersons to come, and it also echoes the four corners of the Earth. As for the interior of the bookshop itself,' he continues, 'that's designed around a compass, with a circular window in the roof and the four points visible when you look up at the sky. Now, when Aziraphale was in Eden he was a guard on the Eastern Gate, and in his bookshop his office is located at the eastern side of the building.'

With a raft of references embedded into the set, from the mystical and occult to religious iconography from across the ages, is Michael concerned that any message may become noise? 'There is a huge amount of symbolism in there,' he agrees, 'but everything substantiates Aziraphale's character. Maybe somebody will look hard and try to decipher it, and there are many levels of discoverability, but for most viewers it'll go to the back of their heads and they won't process it. Even so,' he says, pausing to stress what he has to add next.

Window shopping. Aziraphale's bookshop was built within a detailed recreation of a Soho street block complete with different shopfronts.

The Soho set comes
alive with closely
choreographed
extras populating the
pavements for a scene
featuring Crowley and
his beloved Bentley.

'*I have to know it. If I can dress the set to an extent that there's a spirit there that isn't really me any more then I'll know I've done it right.*'

In overseeing the building of the set, on an airfield adjacent to a prison, Michael jokes that his construction crew were prepared for all eventualities. 'We had to dig a lot of holes,' he says, 'and so at any time we were wondering if we might knock into an escape tunnel. Had any prisoners then popped their heads up they'd look around, see Soho and think they'd come a bit far.'

With a great deal of action taking place in and around Aziraphale's Soho bookshop, it fell to Cesco Reidy to create a schedule that captured everything within a short timeframe. 'Ideally, we would've been shooting in July with nice long days,' he says. 'Obviously in December we were limited with our daylight. This became a real problem for me until Gavin came to the rescue. He worked out a way of floating lights above the set in enormous helium balloons suspended from cranes. So when the sun went down and the real world became dark, the balloons would rise up and throw enough light into the street to create daylight during darkness hours. It meant we could literally turn the night on and off. It was unusual, but then everything in *Good Omens* is about scale.'

Bovingdon Airfield in Hertfordshire hosted the purpose-built Soho set, which was enhanced with green-screen boards to extend the streets in post-production, and floodlights floated from giant helium balloons.

As well as daylight, Cesco needed to populate the streets surrounding Aziraphale's bookstore. This is Soho, after all; a London quarter defined by the never-ending bustle of people and city traffic.

'Michael Ralph's set allowed me to run vehicles through the street and round the back of it, which meant I was able to create any kind of traffic I wanted. I had fifty cars available to me, and each one had a driver on a radio so I was able to speak to them all simultaneously. With the help of my team, I had complete control at the press of a button, and could make the traffic flow or create a jam. Then of course there were the pedestrians,' he adds, and goes on to explain how a seemingly random crowd movement requires careful management for the camera. 'There are systems whereby we break pedestrians into different groups on the pavement. Then we train them to move in circuits, so once filming begins they start to move and will continue in a circular route until I stop them. We also needed a system to randomize people to make it look completely authentic. We wanted to see people walking slowly and talking. People walking on their own and not talking; others on their mobile phones; some standing; others running; and so it goes on.'

Continuing Michael Ralph's circle motif, Aziraphale's bookshop rug hides a cabalistic circle.

About three hundred extras were needed to make this work, Cesco explains. 'They all know the basic circular routine, but then you begin to pick off subgroups based on month of birth, for example, assign them an additional task like talking on a phone, and effectively randomize elements of the system at a single cue. It's very satisfying!' he adds. 'It also contributes something to the look of the show, and we were all so grateful to the supporting cast. They are a very important part of any production.'

As well as enabling the camera to move in ways that shooting on location might not have permitted, and providing complete control over the street life, the production team had one more major reason for building the Soho set.

'The bookshop had to burn down,' says Jemima Thomas. 'We could've done it with visual effects but it wouldn't have had the same impact. Douglas wanted a real fire, and we couldn't do that in Soho.'

Responsibility for the bookshop blaze fell to the special effects supervisor Danny Hargreaves. Like everyone else in the cast and crew as filming at Bovingdon progressed, he had come to appreciate the scale and detail invested in the set by Michael Ralph.

Aziraphale prepares to summon the Metatron – *Good Omens'* floating-headed spokesperson for the Almighty, played by Derek Jacobi.

'I went from being just a guy on set to being the bad guy,' he laughs as the man appointed to set fire to it. 'It also broke my heart a little bit as there were thousands of books, tapestries and beautiful grandfather clocks inside the shop that were real.'

Having begun his career working on the ITV fire brigade drama, *London's Burning*, Danny has a great deal of experience in staging fires for film and television. Perhaps unsurprisingly, on the set of *Good Omens*, preparing to burn down Aziraphale's beloved store, he found himself alongside other graduates from the series.

'Douglas and I also both worked on *London's Burning*,' says Cesco, who is clearly comfortable filming with fire but also well aware of the planning involved to ensure the safety of cast and crew. 'The fact that the set will be burned must be built into the consideration of the design, and Michael did a brilliant job. In terms of preparation, we had to leave the set for a few days so Danny and his guys could rig it with gas lines and flame bars. Each line is linked to its own cylinder, and the feed levels closely supervized at all times.'

'Everything is under control,' Danny points out, 'but there is a limit as to where that fire can go, and we took it right to that limit. The burn time inside the bookshop was quite long, because David Tennant had to do a whole scene in there. Now, as Crowley is from Hell that means fire is his thing. So David had to be very cool about being in there, and he did it so well. The radial heat coming out was incredible, and there were moments where I shut off the gas lines sooner rather than later. One time Douglas came out and questioned why I'd cut it. I had to point out that the roof was about to catch fire.'

Danny points out that the world of VFX also forced him to ensure that the blaze stayed in check. 'Keeping the green screens clear meant we could only go so high with the smoke and flames but we got it done, and my team guaranteed the fire was safely managed at all times.'

As the individual responsible for creating such a magical set, Michael Ralph considers the burn to be just another purpose for its existence.

'What we're doing is supporting the actor,' he says, 'and the emotion around that actor. The set is monstrous, *huge*, but it isn't the show.'

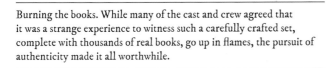

Burning the books. While many of the cast and crew agreed that it was a strange experience to witness such a carefully crafted set, complete with thousands of real books, go up in flames, the pursuit of authenticity made it all worthwhile.

HEAVEN AND HELL

In which we discover that the ultimate stairway is in fact an escalator, and doesn't just lead upwards.

It's a little-known fact that both Heaven and Hell are accessed via the same lobby. A least that's how Neil's vision plays out in his adaptation of *Good Omens*. It was also something that evolved from the script when the location manager Nick Marshall, took Douglas Mackinnon, Michael Ralph and other key crew members on a search for a suitable entrance to the afterlife.

'Douglas and Michael decided to go for something upmarket in the city of London,' says Nick. 'We considered the Shard, and then visited Broadgate Tower on Bishopsgate.'

As soon as they entered the building, continues first assistant director Cesco Reidy, an idea took shape that was driven by imagination and underpinned by technical expertise. 'It's one of those modern, huge, very expensive steel and wire buildings, inside of which companies valued at millions of pounds conduct their business,' he says. 'Standing inside this magnificent lobby, Douglas and Michael realized the shiny marble floor reflected the escalators moving up into the body of the building. It had the effect of creating a mirror image, and this led to an idea that when one person goes up the escalator to Heaven, the other person steps onto one that seemingly drops down into Hell.'

It was a concept that required consultation with *Good Omens'* visual effects supervisor Jean-Claude 'JC' Deguara, one of the founders of the Academy and BAFTA award-winning visual-effects company Milk VFX.

'I'm in two camps, which is the real world and computer graphics,' says the man who would oversee the impression that hellbound travellers literally descend through the floor. 'VFX is not about sitting around waiting for the material. We have to be there in the early stages, planning shots and getting them correct.'

Michael Ralph conjured up the concept of escalators ascending to Heaven and descending to Hell.

The location team found the perfect lobby in a City of London landmark. While Aziraphale and the angels made a simple ascension to the blessed upper floors, Douglas combined real-time cinematography with visual effects to deliver Crowley and his kind from the lobby to the basement depths of Hell.

Throughout the shoot, in fact, JC was a regular presence behind the director's monitors. While Douglas was committed to capturing as much action as possible 'in camera', almost every scene would require some element of post-production visual effects to create a world that is both recognizable and fantastical.

'In simple terms, we put a green screen in the background,' says JC, whose VFX credits include *The Martian*, *Jonathan Strange and Mr Norrell* and *Fantastic Beasts and Where to Find Them*. 'In post-production, this allows us to key out that area so that we can manipulate the image digitally.' In *Good Omens*, Milk VFX's input can range from the extension of a street opposite Aziraphale's bookshop to Episode Four's fast-moving and mindblowing sequence in which one of the Dukes of Hell chases Crowley through the internet.

'We can have anything from sixty to a hundred people working on one of our sequences,' JC adds, to underline the scope of the process. Meanwhile in the lobby, watching Crowley seamlessly sink into the depths while Aziraphale ascends the escalator towards Heaven, it's clear that a visit to Broadgate Tower will never be the same again.

Like any big organization, Heaven requires an administration level. Managed by divine office drones such as Sandalphon, Uriel and Michael, martialled by the Quartermaster Angel and overseen by Jon Hamm's Gabriel, the heavenly afterlife is run with ruthless efficiency. It was up to Michael Ralph and Douglas Mackinnon to create a memorable floor for the archangel to command.

'We found a vacant office building in a smart business park in Weybridge, Surrey,' says location manager Nick Marshall. 'It had a tiled floor, white pillars and 132 floor-to-ceiling windows. We had to frost every single one of them to get the light looking celestial,' he adds. 'It really did have a heavenly vibe.'

Producer Phil Collinson notes that the sheer scale of the floor space lifted the corporate mundanity into another dimension. 'It was like an office that goes on forever whichever way you turned, and yet there was something tangible about it. You felt like this was a place where people might work.'

With the space prepared, Cesco Reidy explains how they went on to populate it with an appropriate workforce.

'We had the supporting artists in angel outfits,' he says, 'but instead of them walking around we provided them with hoverboards so they appeared to glide. It wasn't appropriate to make it a big feature, but as a background subtlety it was one of those things that provided beautiful results. We didn't hide the hoverboards, and that was part of the charm.'

In keeping with traditional office hierarchy, the upper floor of Heaven is the most exclusive. While God may be on a higher level, and kindly serving as the series narrator, this had to be a place where beatific boardroom decisions could be made by an archangel and his colleagues. On locating a sky garden with views over the capital, and with the help of the VFX supervisor, production designer Michael Ralph allowed his imagination to soar.

'It had to be mind-blowing,' he says. 'The best real estate in the world. So they're up in the clouds but on Earth. Then I had this idea that they should be looking out across the city – and not just the city of London but *every* city. So we see the Eiffel Tower, the Pyramids, the Chrysler Building, the twin towers of Singapore, and it's constantly changing. It provides a view that nobody has ever seen before.'

In keeping with the originality of portraying Heaven as a sublime corporate headquarters, the team envisioned Hell as a realm that did away with the traditional iconography of eternal damnation.

'There's no fire,' says director of photography Gavin Finney. 'It's just crappy.'

You know that time in any big building when you head for the ground floor and accidentally take one flight too many? That moment when you open the fire doors into a network of dingy and claustrophobic service corridors that smell of mould? Well, that's Hell, and HQ for eternal wretches Hastur, Ligur, Dagon and Beelzebub .

Producer Phil Collinson reasons that Hell in *Good Omens* is effectively a reflection of the occupant's status.

'God and the angels got the pick of the best place,' he says, 'while the demons go down into the basement. Hell is like a struggling business that can't afford a bigger premises. Nothing works properly and it could do with a paint job.'

Filmed in Cape Town, the crew located a former abattoir as a suitably grim underworld space. To illustrate the torture of existing in Hell, Neil Gaiman created motivational posters for the walls. 'I had too much fun with these,' he

A Heavenly view. Michael Ralph envisioned the top floor to be the finest real estate on the planet. To reflect this, he created an ever-changing view of skylines from around the world, as seen here in this early concept design.

WE HATE YOU

The Devil Finds WORK FOR IDLE HANDS TO DO - so LOOK BUSY!

For More Efficient Service just rip out your own throat with a stapler

You DON'T MATTER

With Neil's understated comic vision as a foundation, Michael Ralph constructed an underworld furnished with plastic chairs, bad lighting and poor ventilation, along with demotivational posters personally penned by the screenwriter himself.

says. 'The hardest part was just persuading the art department that I was serious about getting them to forget everything they had ever learned about design.'

According to Cesco Reidy, it was the physical shape of the abattoir that went on to inform the scene.

'Within the building there is an auction area where the buyers of the meat used to sit on tiers of stone steps. At the bottom, on the auction floor, is an opening about the size of a small cinema screen. The meat would be brought through and people would bid on the lot. For our purposes, the shape of this room lent itself to the idea that if we put a glass sheet over the opening then we could see the demons of Hell pressed up against it. We had over one hundred supporting actors in for a big scene with David Tennant. It was inventive and fun.'

In many ways, this awful, soul-destroying environment is more hellish than anything previously attempted on screen, as Michael Ralph agrees.

'All you hear is the opening and closing of doors,' he laughs. 'People are lost. There's rubbish in the corners and lights hanging out of the ceiling, and if you go in for an interview there's a card table with two mismatched chairs. That's their world. And it's fantastic.'

Over a hundred intricately made-up extras filled the viewing area of a disused abbatoir, creating a hellishly claustrophobic scene.

GABRIEL

JON HAMM

'We live in a time in which everyone is so convinced that their side is right. But the more you look at it, the more you realize that both sides are ridiculous in their certainty, and that the truth lies in the middle.'

With a cup of black coffee in hand and news footage on the TV behind him of forest fires back home in California, Jon Hamm has just outlined to me how *Good Omens* could work as an analogy for the polarity between Republicans and Democrats in America's current political scene. The *Mad Men* star is smartly dressed, fully engaged in his subject and keen to talk about his role in the screen adaptation as God's alpha angel, Gabriel.

'If anything, this might be the century in which we figure out that the truth lies in the middle,' he says. 'If we can just get through it and not blow each other up.'

It's a view that Aziraphale and Crowley might share, unlike the archangel whose patience with Michael Sheen's angel thins as the story progresses.

'Gabriel is barely in the novel,' Jon continues, 'but he's fleshed out here because Neil Gaiman wanted someone cracking the whip. So he's the guy from head office who is like, "Hey, what are you doing? Go to work!" As a narrative device it's very funny, and the fact that I get to do it is awesome because originally he was written as being British,' Jon continues. 'That stuffy, posh Brit who can't get out of his own way. But then Neil felt he should be from the USA, and that made sense to me. The idea of the American walking in and saying: "We gotta do it my way!" is very easy for me to inhabit.'

Like so many members of the cast, Jon Hamm joined the *Good Omens* production with a longstanding passion for the story. 'I was a Neil Gaiman fan from comics,' he says. 'As a bit of an anglophile, I like British fantasy and sci-fi,

An empty floor of an office building in Weybridge, Surrey, transformed with window frosting, careful lighting and a lot of polish into the pristine administrative level of Heaven. Here, Aziraphale reports in to Gabriel and his angelic executive team.

GABRIEL: I would like to purchase one of your material objects.

and so in novels like *American Gods* and *Good Omens* I just appreciated his ability to write stories at an elevated, intelligent level in which your knowledge and cleverness are rewarded. What Neil and Terry have done is create a world and then say, "Come along for this great ride, and if you know a little bit more about certain things then it'll be better. You don't have to know all the references we're giving you, but you can look them up if you like." Now, I was always a well-read kid, and I got it. That was the exciting part for me.'

Like his previous incarnation, fifties' advertising executive Don Draper, Jon Hamm's Gabriel is a company man mixing business with pleasure. As well as on the office floor, we encounter this modern-day archangel in a sushi restaurant and jogging through St James's Park, and yet even out of the office he's singing from the corporate hymn sheet. In many ways, Heaven is portrayed not so much as a higher state but as a powerful entity from our capitalist age.

'It's a multinational corporation representing good, not representing humanity,' explains Jon. 'They have their own interests, while humanity is a thing they developed to get to Armageddon. The whole point of creating Earth

Gabriel visits A. Z. Fell and Co. with his thuggish sidekick Sandalphon (Paul Chahidi) to inform Aziraphale of the preparations that are in play for the upcoming Armageddon.

is to have the war between good and evil. So you have this perfect angelic team but they're just as bad, conniving or double dealing as they are in Hell. They do everything very nicely and politely, but the knives are out under the jacket. And that's the tone of the thing. We're all imperfect. Even the people who are perfectly good and perfectly evil are imperfect, and Crowley and Aziraphale realize this. Having been on Earth for so long, they appreciate our messed-up imperfections. And the great irony in the story is that the people who are tasked with living among humanity are those who end up liking humanity more than they like the perfect derivations of their team – of evil and of good. The wonder of life is living in the grey, not the black and the white. It's a lovely thing, and they've come to enjoy moving among it in an elevated way. They don't want to end it, simply because it's written.'

The notion that our destiny must be set in stone is something Terry Pratchett and Neil Gaiman explore throughout *Good Omens*, often to comic effect. Jon also appreciates the rich seam of humour to be mined from such rigid thinking.

'Gabriel is a team player, but it's his team. He reports to the big boss,' he says, pointing upwards, 'and yet he's the captain; some shady boss who won't listen to you, and insists you have to do something because it's written down. That's the universality that I really enjoyed about it. Everyone has that person in their life who just won't listen to reality or the facts on the ground. Instead, these are the rules and there's no deviation from that. These are people who can't live outside the box. Their whole world *is* the box.'

For an archangel, Jon Hamm's Gabriel does away with the huge, folding wings in favour of a unique look. 'Our costume designer, Claire, is phenomenal. She told me, "I just want you to look perfect." I said, "OK. What are you thinking? Like a robe or something?" and she replied, "No, a bespoke, beautiful suit and coat that's tailor-made for you." I said, "Well, we're in London. We can probably find somebody to do that!" and so we went to Bond Street. Claire picked out all the fabric, and said, "I want it light, ethereal, ephemeral, like you just walked into it." I think she got it right,' he adds.

With the costume complete, hair and make-up designer Nosh Oldham finished the look of an angel with an agenda. 'Jon is a handsome man,' she says,

An early costume design by Claire Anderson, emphasising Gabriel's fine sense of taste and lilac colour theme.

GABRIEL: Lose the gut. You're a lean, mean fighting machine. What are you?

Filming well-known actors like Jon Hamm and Michael Sheen in public spaces such as St James's Park required careful planning, organisation and security – not easy for a large-scale production such as *Good Omens*.

'and that made me think of Elizabeth Taylor, one of the most beautiful women in the world. So I gave him lilac eyes; lenses based on Taylor's colouring, which worked really well with the blue-grey suit.'

The outfit is one that Jon says helped him to finesse his character. He refers to a scene in which Gabriel checks up on Aziraphale's bid to steer the impending apocalypse in Heaven's favour. While reminding the angel and bookseller of his duty, he laments the fact that it means he'll miss his suit. 'The one thing Gabriel really likes about Earth is the tailors,' says Jon. 'Which works on a funny level as he's a little narcissistic in that way. He likes to look good.'

Jon Hamm's turn as the uncompromising archangel shows an actor with a deep appreciation for British humour. Gabriel is quietly menacing and yet wholly unaware of his flaws, which combines to brilliant effect. 'Everyone is working at an extremely high level and it inspires me. It's like playing tennis against someone who is really good. Now you don't want to suck. You don't want to be the one who stinks, and so it raises your own game. But the great thing about it is that if you're a fan of Neil and Terry you're going to love it. That's all I can say, because I'm a fan of the book, and proud to be a part of it.'

Confused by Aziraphale, political enemies Gabriel and Beelzebub can only turn to each other as their confidence in the Great Plan fades.

THE DUKES OF HELL

NED DENNEHY – *HASTUR*
ARIYON BAKARE – *LIGUR*

'Arguably the only two actually evil characters
in the whole thing are Hastur and Ligur,'
observes Douglas Mackinnon.

 If *Good Omens* is about blurring the boundaries between darkness and light, there is little such grey area for the two Dukes of Hell charged with delivering the Antichrist-in-a-basket to Crowley – and then hounding him when it all goes wrong. From the moment we meet them in a graveyard at night, preparing to hand over the goods, it's clear this dastardly duo do not belong in this world. Surfacing throughout the series, tasked as they are with ensuring Armageddon kicks off without a hitch, they make every effort to appear as human and yet somehow their efforts to disguise their demonic origins always fall short.

Hastur and Ligur, played respectively by Ned Dennehy and Ariyon Bakare, are strong on menace but also responsible for moments of exquisite comedy. As *Good Omens* addresses the question of how many angels can dance on the head of a pin, which sees the pair imagined in a surreal disco groove, their roles are both inventive and hugely original. In some ways, it's a surprise and a delight when Ned claims to have a blueprint for his part.

'I see Hastur as a tired James Mason who has been in the pub for three days and is on his way home,' he jokes. 'Though I've no idea if James Mason even went to the pub.' Nevertheless, it's a fitting image for Ned's take on his Duke of Hell. 'He's bitter and sarcastic, dry, smug and irritable, and with a total dislike of Crowley,' he adds.

Ned conjures an image of the qualities that embody his character while on a break from filming in London's St James's Park. He's here to shoot a sequence in which Crowley is literally snatched in broad daylight by Hastur

The unholy handover scene, in which the Dukes of Hell present Crowley with the Antichrist child, was shot on location at night in the grounds of Holy Trinity Church near Amersham in Buckinghamshire.

and Ligur and dragged to Hell to answer questions about his allegiance. The actor recognizable for his role as Charlie Strong in the popular BBC twenties' gangster drama, *Peaky Blinders*, is sitting in his production trailer with me, wearing a badly fitting dress and sporting what looks like flecks of mould on his face. It's an image created for him by Claire Anderson and Nosh Oldham. Before he's called on to set, it'll be completed with the application of a prosthetic frog on his head.

'I'm inhabiting a lady tourist's body today,' he explains. 'We do this whenever we rise up from Hell in an attempt to appear human. It's just we're not very good at disguises. So you always find us in various levels of disarray, but the purpose remains the same. That's the hot pursuit of Crowley, and getting Armageddon back on track.'

Ned Dennehy is naturally funny. The Irishman's humour is bone dry, and he's unafraid to laugh at himself. He's also well aware of the reason why he's been cast on the side of evil. 'The angels are whiter than white with clean American looks,' he says. 'They're manicured people, and it's a great look, but I'm not one of those people. I'm straight out of the demon bag.'

Feathered wing stubs were considered for the Dukes of Hell at the costume design stage, before Claire Anderson chose to focus on making both characters look as if their clothing had been scorched from the ground up, inspired by a traditional vision of Hell.

Actors Ned Dennehy and Ariyon Bakare worked closely with hair and make-up designer Nosh Oldham in creating unconventional demons. Here, Ligur sports the chameleon that squats atop his head, while grave-eyed Hastur struggles to contain his infernal identity in human form.

**HASTUR: I'm Hastur...
La Vista... I'm an
archaeologist... which one
of you is the ambassador?**

In their pursuit of Crowley, both Dukes of Hell appear extensively throughout the series. Here, Hastur ventures out to the archaeological site of Megiddo for the first of many satanic setbacks...

Nevertheless Ned can see some light in his character. 'I feel he's just been failed. That somewhere Hastur has been let down, thwarted, and things haven't worked out, and it's one thing after another. Hastur is a proper Pratchett character,' he suggests. 'An angry person with too much to do. So he's towing the company line, and it's a tedious task, but you can't ignore the fact that he has a frog on his head.'

For all the characteristics that define Hastur, a sociable streak is largely absent. This makes the pairing with his fellow Duke of Hell all the more endearing. Ariyon Bakare, plays fellow henchman, Ligur. He sees his character as a demon who is capable of greater acts of evil. 'Hastur has more of a heart,' he says, 'but Ligur is really gone. I asked myself what he'd done way back that was so bad that he went to Hell. In my mind, I feel he was some eighteenth-century gangster who died riddled with bullet holes.'

Despite their demonic differences, Ariyon recognizes that Ligur and Hastur are united in their mission to bring Crowley to task and share many qualities. 'They are cut from the same cloth,' he says, 'and if you're both in Hell for eternity

then it stands to reason that you need someone to connect with.' As Hastur has his frog, Ariyon's Duke of Hell appears on screen with a chameleon on his head.

'It changes colour with Ligur's emotions,' he tells me. 'Nosh had lots of pictures to show me when we were creating the look. I latched onto a shot of a man with his hair shaved into the shape of a lizard, and that's when the idea of a chameleon emerged. Nosh just ran with it, and the next thing I know I'm in prosthetics getting it all done. It was just a lovely thing we created together.'

Crowned by these strange, squatting creatures, the actors serve up a formidable double act. They also forged a friendship off screen that thrives on a quality of banter that could have been in existence for a lifetime. 'We finish each other's sentences like a husband and wife,' jokes Ariyon, and then grins playfully when he describes their first encounter at the read-through. 'I remember thinking there was no way I could work with this guy. He looked so mardy, and came across like an Irishman with all the charm switched off.' He pauses there, and then gives his fellow Duke of Hell more serious consideration. 'The truth is working with Ned has been a highlight. He really goes for it. His reactions are big. I wish I was as brave as him as an actor.'

Hastur may struggle to mask his demonic identity, but even when badly disguised as a tourist it seems that Crowley didn't see him coming.

BEELZEBUB

ANNA MAXWELL MARTIN

'As Beelzebub, I am answerable to Satan. My kids don't know what I'm doing in *Good Omens* but I will tell them how powerful I was and they will get into line.'

The actress Anna Maxwell Martin laughs with unnerving glee. From the moment she talks about her role as one of the top dogs in Hell, it's clear she relished the part. While she can only hope that her children will fall into step, on screen Anna commands absolute deference and respect from Hastur, Ligur and the wretched legions of the underworld.

With her wild wig, which she describes as 'like the late, great Ken Dodd', pustulous spots and a helix of flies buzzing around her, Anna Maxwell Martin's Beelzebub is a sight to behold. Inevitably the transformation into a satanic wretch involved long stints in the make-up chair.

'I'm not good with make-up,' she says. 'Anything longer than twenty minutes and I start to fidget, so it was a struggle for me to sit there for an hour, but *Good Omens* is such a huge production and that was the nature of the beast.'

Like Hastur, Ligur and her fellow cursed souls, Beelzebub was dressed in clothing that had been carefully blackened and shredded at the hems.'They've come from Hell,' explains costume designer Claire Anderson. 'So it looks as if they've been scorched from below.'

'Beelzebub has a great sense of self and a pomposity about her,' says Anna. 'She stomps around shouting a lot, but I don't play her as scary,' she adds.

On screen, Anna Maxwell Martin's Beelzebub is a compelling presence. In keeping with Douglas's approach, Anna plays the role straight and allows the comedy to emerge from the absurdity of a moment or scene. Despite the assurance of her performance, she admits to being nervous about how to portray Satan's right-hand woman.

No flies on her.
Anna Maxwell
Martin's Beelzebub
listens sceptically
to Crowley's phony
progress report on
preparations for
Armageddon.

'I was approached to play the role. There was no audition, and so it can be tricky knowing what to do. When you just turn up on set, it can be frightening to think you might try out something and everyone just laughs at you. Fortunately, that didn't happen,' she adds. 'Douglas knows what he wants, and is so focused and calm, but then he has to be on such a massive show. He was on top of it, and that gives me confidence as an actor.'

Anna's character in *Good Omens* is undoubtedly a departure from her previous appearances on stage and screen, including her recent starring role as a harassed mum in the BBC's comedy *Motherland*. She freely admits that she's never done anything like it both in terms of character and also the sheer scale of the production. Nevertheless the actor summons her inner fiend with memorable effect.

'I was worried that the Hell scenes shot in the abattoir would mean blood in the gutter and stinky meat everywhere,' she confesses with her tongue in cheek. 'I'm semi-vegetarian, and that wouldn't have been good for me, but it was nothing like that. It was just a fabulous experience and the chance to work with an amazing cast.'

BEELZEBUB: But the battle must be decided now, boy. That is your deztiny. It is written. Now: start the war.

Forced into the light. Beelzebub's ascension to the airbase transforms her into an almost human form. During post-production the Milk VFX team will digitally unleash flies to buzz around her.

WARLOCK COMES OF AGE

In which the demon and the angel discover that working with children isn't just challenging for mortals.

'The kids have a big pie fight at the end, which was fun. The hardest bit was getting them to stop. It was easier to manage a bookshop fire than forty-eight pie-throwing children.'

Good Omens' producer Phil Collinson smiles to himself as he reflects on the shoot for an ambitious scene referred to by cast and crew as 'The Birthday Party'. It takes place in the grounds of the American ambassador's residence, inside a huge marquee. Here, surrounded by excitable friends, the ambassador's son, Warlock, is celebrating turning eleven. Through the eyes of Crowley and Aziraphale, unaware that Sister Mary Loquacious made a mess of the baby swap when she was handed the Son of Satan all those years ago, this is the Antichrist child. More immediately, the boy has reached the age at which he's set to fulfil his destiny. Having shadowed his upbringing, and each quietly schooled him in the merits of the middle ground they have come to enjoy through life on Earth, both the demon and the angel feel sure Warlock will skip kick-starting Armageddon and thereby spare the world.

The hitch is that Warlock is not the boy they believe him to be. If anything, as the brat in question turns his birthday celebrations into bedlam, he's worse than the Antichrist that Crowley and Aziraphale have somehow mislaid.

'He's spoiled and rude. Just not a nice kid,' says the young actor tasked with playing the American ambassador's son. Unlike his character, Warlock Dowling, Samson Marraccino has a sharp sense of humour and is unafraid to laugh at himself. 'It didn't take that much effort to get in the zone,' he continues, talking about his role with his mother alongside him. 'I have a lifetime of experience.'

'He's not that similar,' his mum is quick to point out. 'But we could see how he might get there.'

Warlock's lavish cake represents what Neil and Douglas intended to be the best birthday party the son of an American ambassador could wish for.

Being a bad children's party magician isn't as easy as it looks, though Michael Sheen's Aziraphale puts in a flawless performance with young Warlock looking on.

It's hard to see how any unpleasant streak comes naturally to this bright and engaging young actor. Samson credits a meeting with director Douglas Mackinnon as the opportunity for him to step up as a character who sorely deserves time out on the naughty step.

'Douglas just said that he believed in me,' Samson says cheerily. 'So I tried out different ways to say the same line until I found a way to be bratty.'

Samson also credits the script with helping him to define his character. 'Warlock has to react to lots of things,' he says. 'He also has some excellent lines.'

For a boy whose age is barely in double figures, Samson Marraccino's turn as the kind of unpleasant kid who'd earn Willy Wonka's displeasure showcases a young acting talent with huge potential. In talking to Samson, it's also clear that he handled himself with great maturity when faced with an experience in front of the camera that many of his peers might have found overwhelming.

'I got to work with David and Michael, which was amazing,' he says. 'And Neil Gaiman was so nice, though it must've been weird for him because he invented me in his mind.'

True to form, *Good Omens* pays no heed to the unspoken rules of filming that warn against working with children and animals. While the creatures come later, Samson and the other kids that populate this scene are actively encouraged to behave like monkeys. For a producer overseeing the smooth running of the set, Phil Collinson considers arming children with pies as just another day in an extraordinary shoot.

'It's a massive beast,' he says. 'Just full on. I'd worked on the *Doctor Who* reboot with Russell T. Davies, and ran *Coronation Street* for three years that included the tram crash storyline. So, I like to do the big stuff,' he adds with a grin, and in a way that makes it come across like an understatement.

By his own admission, *Good Omens* is the most ambitious screen venture that Phil has ever steered. How does he navigate a shoot involving dozens of excitable children and remain as calm and good-natured as he comes across?

'I'm like a swan,' he jokes. 'I have to be seen to be benevolent and everyone's friend, but underneath the water I'm pedalling frantically. So I'm a real believer in letting people do their jobs, and getting on with what they do best. My role

Warlock's birthday party took place in the grounds of a house that would befit an American ambassador to the UK. Despite shooting on an overcast day in October 2017, the crew worked hard to light the scene to create a summer atmosphere.

is about making sure the mechanics of the production are working *behind* the scenes,' he continues. 'So that on the day the lights are on and the cameras are rolling and everyone is as happy as they can possibly be.'

So, while Douglas Mackinnon and his crew orchestrate the onset of a pie fight, how does Phil ensure that everyone is free to focus on the task at hand?

'I'm there to protect the director and the showrunner,' he says, 'so they can get on with realizing the vision with as little compromise as possible. The producer is effectively a buffer,' he adds. 'It means I get to dip into everything from set design to props, stunts, prosthetics and costume. From the perspective of budgets, it's about encouraging people to look at different ways of doing things in order to get it done.'

As a producer on a show of this scale, does Phil see a risk that he'll be stuck in the production trailer trawling through piles of paperwork?

'If I'm not careful,' he agrees with a smile, 'which is why I need to be on set as much as on the phone to executives and agents. The fact is people want to see the producer as a creative entity, a figurehead for the crew, and not someone who is just ticking boxes.'

In this respect, Phil is a producer who seeks to make sure that his budget is spent in a way that every penny has a tangible impact on the quality of the production. 'We sit in our living rooms with these huge televisions,' he says, 'and so it's becoming a more cinematic medium. We're also watching on laptops and tablets, which only increases the appetite for content. There's no going back, and it's great for the industry, but it also means we have to become bolder. *Good Omens* is a big-budget show,' he says by way of example. 'It isn't just about special effects and visual effects. It's also characterful. And so my challenge is to deliver that and make sure there is as much of the money on screen as possible.'

As the birthday boy is the son of a US ambassador, production designer Michael Ralph set out to make this a bash that befitted the family's status.

'It was such a beautiful house and grounds that we desperately wanted it to feel like a rich boy's party,' he says of the shoot on location in Borehamwood, north-west of London. 'So we put up marquees and had carousels with mirrors that flicked the light around.'

Before the party really started, however, the *Good Omens* crew worked hard to cover all the shots they needed that didn't involve low-flying trifles.

'All the chaotic stuff got left to the end of the day,' says script supervisor Jemima Thomas. 'Douglas made sure he got everything else first,' she adds, and references Michael Sheen's turn as an angel disguised as a party magician whose wholesome act earns disdain from Warlock and his guests, and then finally a barrage of biscuits, cake and crisps. 'If we'd done the food fight early it would've required massive changes.'

According to first assistant director Cesco Reidy, it wasn't just planning that proved key to making sure that a shoot involving excitable kids didn't descend into chaos. It also demanded a genuine willingness to work with young actors and make the experience as enjoyable as possible.

'When my children were growing up, I liked nothing more than putting up a big marquee in the garden and inviting their friends around for a party,' says Cesco. 'Filming with children isn't that much different in the way that you communicate with them. You see that they're happy and comfortable, that they

understand what's required of them and enjoy the experience, which is key in my view.'

So, when it comes to inviting nearly fifty kids to start a food fight, how did Cesco maintain the control required to get the job done?

'By providing them with an environment in which if they did get carried away nothing untoward could happen,' he laughs. 'So basically we chose very soft food for ammunition like tiny cream cakes and cucumber sandwiches made on soft white bread. I also gave them a safety talk beforehand, and explained to them that we were trying to convey the look of a food fight that was chaotically funny rather than chaotically scary.'

For Samson Marraccino and co, this was an opportunity to take part in a scene most kids could only dream about.

'We had just watched Michael's magic show,' he begins. 'It's supposed to be really bad, which I think must be quite hard to do, and that's when the fight starts. We just went for it with trifle, juice in cups, the lot!' As the child at the heart of the action, Samson explains how his character came under fire. 'We weren't allowed to aim for Michael or David, but the other kids were allowed to

The US Secret Service under deep cover to keep the ambassador and his family safe. If only they knew a demon was in their midst...

target me,' he says. 'My best technique was to aim for their heads with cups of juice as soon as the food fight began, but I still got hit in the face by a trifle.'

In reliving the action blow by blow, Samson appears to need to remind himself that the fight was in fact staged. 'We were good at stopping whenever the director shouted "Cut!"' he says eventually. 'In between takes, some people were like, "Yeah, we're doing another one!" and others were saying, "I'm cold. I want to go home!" but I didn't mind being covered in food,' he laughs, and goes on to claim it was one of his best filming days ever. 'I'm like a food-fight expert now,' he declares proudly. 'I know what to throw at people and what to dodge. It's a nice skill!' he finishes. Beside him, his mother makes no comment.

In orchestrating the event, Cesco credits Samson and the young actors around him with recognizing their responsibilities in shooting the scene successfully. For all the fun and games, they got the job done.

The result is a sequence that shows how working with a young cast can be fun, effective and highly entertaining. As for Aziraphale and Crowley, now the realization has dawned on them that the brat they've been watching over is not the Antichrist child, this is one birthday party they'd like to forget.

In staging an authentic food fight that guaranteed nobody got hurt, first assistant director Cesco Reidy armed the young actors with soft ammunition: cake and crustless cucumber sandwiches.

IN HOGBACK WOOD

In which an idyllic childhood haunt becomes a court for the Antichrist child and the scene for several stunts.

'*Good Omens* is not a war movie, but for me it feels like one!'

Stunt coordinator Cedric Proust looks exhausted. He's taken a rare moment away from filming to discuss his role, and slumps on a sofa with his baseball cap in his lap. For someone who has worked on big-budget action hits like *Inception*, *Gladiator* and *Mission Impossible*, surely a television series about a laid-back demon and his angelic bookseller associate shouldn't be too much of a stretch? Cedric begs to differ.

'In particular, my role is about safety,' says the Moroccan-born Cedric. 'In *Good Omens* that involves stunts with kids. I'm used to working on big action scenes, but often it's much harder to pull off stunts that aren't action-orientated, and involve real actors, like having four children on wires. In a way,' he adds, 'it's more complicated than sending two hundred soldiers on horseback into battle.'

Cedric Proust is referencing a key scene that takes place in the kind of idyllic rural hideaway where childhood friendships are forged. Here in Hogback Wood, four youngsters known collectively as the Them spend their days at play. Principled tomboy Pepper, serious-minded Wensleydale and grubby but good-hearted Brian each bring unique qualities to the gang, which is led by eleven-year-old Adam Young. Adam is a charismatic dreamer. He's also about to discover that he is in fact the Son of Satan, with powers to shape the world around him.

The trouble is that thanks to his normal upbringing in a perfect English village he's just too grounded and nice to take advantage of the situation. Take the hell-hound waiting in the undergrowth to serve at his side. This slathering beast should strike fear into the hearts of Adam's friends, only for it to emerge

Michael Ralph's production design illustration of the Them's woodland idyll, complete with a makeshift throne, echoes classic childhood meeting places from *Just William* to *The Goonies*.

The Them
innocently play fight
in Hogback Wood,
little knowing the
recently released
hell-hound is
watching them from
the trees, waiting for
his master's summons.

as a loveable little lapdog when the boy describes the kind of pooch he'd most like for his birthday. The sequence, largely handled by Milk VFX, succeeds in being both menacing and comic, while the drama that unfolds within this leafy glade goes on to see Adam and his friends literally suspended in the air above the treetops.

'It was down to me to figure out how to do it,' says Cedric. 'So we had a big crane with wires and harnesses, which lifted each kid about fifty feet into the air. That's some height for a child, and a big challenge for me,' he continues. 'On screen, levitation looks easy, but it's quite an art. The wires pull, which means we need holes in the clothes, but even then certain anchor points can be visible so I need to work with the VFX guys who can cover it up in post-production. There's also pressure from the harness,' he continues, 'and the actors really need to feel comfortable. So we could only keep them in the air for a short while each time. We know the risks, which is why we have one stunt rigger dedicated to working with each child.' Cedric pauses there, points to the sky above the woods and smiles in recollection, 'Meanwhile, they're up there having the time of their lives.'

Shot on location in an old bomb crater in Painshill Park, Surrey, the Them's hideaway is contained by steep, sloping banks that deliberately echo the walls around the Garden of Eden. It forms the perfect place for Adam and his hell-hound to hang out with his friends.

New to the area and finding her bearings, Anathema Device comes across the Them playing a game they call the British Inquisition.

On screen, the result is both charming and breathtaking. It also looks very natural, as the kids float over the treetops and implore their friend with the fiendish new powers to set them down. In Cedric's opinion, this is key to a job well done.

'A good stunt is invisible,' he says. 'You don't notice it. There are no huge stunts in *Good Omens* but lots that fit the story. It might be a little fight or a punch, and so you can't get into some crazy martial arts sequence. It's been hard to make it all work,' he adds, and pops his cap back with the bill pulled low, ready to rejoin the set. 'But I've loved it.'

Another significant challenge for Cedric and the whole crew was the location for Hogback Wood.

'We went to Painshill Park in Surrey,' says producer Phil Collinson. 'It's a beautiful place, but tough to service a shoot there as we were buried in the middle of woodland. So we had to use golf carts and small vehicles for the cast, crew and all the kit. It was like bringing in a circus.'

While access was an issue, it was the scouting party who recognized that a peculiarity of the location lent itself to the story. 'A bomb had dropped there during the Second World War,' explains first assistant director Cesco Reidy. 'It left a huge crater between some large trees.'

According to the location manager Nick Marshall, all agreed that in the right hands it could become the Hogback Wood that the story required. 'The crater was the perfect oasis for a set designer to create a paradise,' he says, which is where Michael Ralph came into his own.

'As soon as I saw a photograph,' says Michael, referring to a shot of the proposed location, 'I knew the crater would be significant. This is where Adam has found his world, his Eden, unaware that he's the Antichrist, and a bomb has gone off here. It was a happy accident!' he declares, before explaining how further subliminal visual strands weave through the show. 'You don't see the "through line" when you read the script,' he says, alluding to the main theme or idea that runs through a piece of work, 'but I have the needle that stitches it all together. You can only do one piece at a time, and one influences the next, but the whole thing comes together as circular storytelling. So, in Hogback

Wood we have the crater, and that mirrors the shape of the Garden of Eden and Aziraphale's bookshop. It's the ball, your eye, a water drop, our Earth, and one of the oldest images in the world of the snake eating its own tail. It's also Yin and Yang,' Michael points out, mindful of Crowley and Aziraphale's relationship as he refers to the Chinese theory of opposing forces coming together to form a whole. 'The circle of life itself.'

With exposed roots added to the crater walls, moss banks and a tree house, Michael and his team created what they imagined to be an ideal world for a young boy and his friends, and invited director of photography Gavin Finney to explore it in full effect.

'We actually rotated the set around so that the sun would be in just the right place at a certain time,' says Gavin. 'We then had lights up on cranes and in trees to create beautiful shafts of sunshine. It was magical.'

As well as creating a paradise in Hogback Wood, the story demanded that the location also came under fire from the elements as Adam channels his satanic powers. 'We had it all planned out,' Gavin continues, 'and shot the storm scenes at the end of the day in lower light.'

While the *Good Omens* production embraced extreme weather conditions, in the UK and South Africa, they couldn't rely on the weather to turn treacherous on cue over Hogback Wood. Here, special effects supervisor Danny Hargreaves explains how he helped to whip up a maelstrom.

'We used a variety of rain machines and trailer-mounted wind machines so that some areas are more intense than others,' he says. 'We also brought in a device called an air mover which allows us to shoot debris like leaves into the scene.' While the Hogback Wood shoot was filmed across an intense six-day period, and with epic results, Danny points out that both the input and outcome is a reflection of telling stories for the small screen today. 'We don't have film and television any more,' he says. 'We have a hybrid, which means we have film resources, such as technocranes and drones, but we still shoot on a TV schedule.' From his tone, and having helped to levitate four children over storm-tossed treetops, Danny is not complaining. 'It means we have more toys to play with,' he says happily.

With Adam levitating a couple of feet from the ground, the Them realise that something is very wrong. While Pepper is angry, Wensleydale and Brian are whimpering, but not for long...

THE THEM

SAM TAYLOR BUCK – *ADAM*
AMMA RIS – *PEPPER*
ILAN GALKOFF – *BRIAN*
ALFIE TAYLOR – *WENSLEYDALE*

'One of my favourite shots of the series is when we find the Them in Hogback Wood,' says script supervisor Jemima Thomas. 'We had a camera on a big wire rig, like a zip wire, and it just flew through the trees to find the children and their den.'

Wires seem to feature heavily for the young actors who play the gang that might one day save the world. Amma Ris, Ilan Galkoff and Alfie Taylor have just descended to the studio floor for a break in filming. They are followed down by Sam Taylor Buck, who plays the gang's leader, a boy who is about to wake to powers that could serve as the final full stop in the history of the world. Under the gentle guidance of director Douglas Mackinnon, they are shooting additional material against a green screen. Despite being suspended in the air over several takes, they come back to earth as if it's second nature to them now.

'Everyone else loved it, but I was shaking,' admits Ilan Galkoff, who plays Brian, when considering how it felt when they first went up on wires. 'You need a lot of core strength, and generally I'm quite a weak person.'

A slight, dark-haired boy with a winning smile, Ilan's admission prompts much laughter from his young fellow cast members. They're well aware that they've landed important roles in a production with huge audience expectation. While it doesn't appear to have fazed them, the way they recount the experience of working on *Good Omens* suggests it has certainly brought them together. In talking to me about their experience on set and on location, reminding each other of memorable moments, they come across as firm friends.

ADAM: I think I'll call him Dog. Saves a lot of trouble, a name like that.

The Antichrist child's best friend. Adam runs with his fearsome hell-hound (trapped inside the body of a friendly pooch).

ADAM: Have you got any more of the New Aquariums? Cos, we need to know everything.

'I've done a lot of musical theatre and small TV projects,' says Ilan, 'but something like this has been amazing. I've learned so much.'

Amma Ris, who plays Pepper, nods in agreement.

'This has been quite relaxed compared to musical theatre,' she says, having appeared in *The Lion King* and *School of Rock*. 'If you make an error on set it's fine. You can just do it again. In theatre, everyone can see!'

'You've got to get your lines right in theatre,' agrees Alfie Taylor, who plays Wensleydale, sounding seasoned beyond his years.

In assembling their gang for *Good Omens*, Terry Pratchett and Neil Gaiman called upon elements of a lost childhood age found in the pages of *Just William* and Enid Blyton's *Famous Five*. Neil has retained that spirit in the television adaptation, while pulling in a contemporary edge that's most apparent in Amma Ris's spirited Pepper.

'She's a strong feminist with an internal fire,' says Amma with some conviction. 'Pepper doesn't like sexism and she's politically aware. It's an easy role for me to play as I have my strong opinions.'

Fortune comes knocking. New to the village of Tadfield, Anathema Device opens the door of her cottage to the Them. The kids are just curious to meet the new resident they've been told is a witch, while Anathema has no idea that one of them is key to her quest to stop the end of the world.

In dressing the Them, Claire Anderson sought to capture a universal spirit of childhood while embodying each character with qualities that linked them to the Horsemen they ultimately battle. From left to right: Adam Young, dressed in strong colours to denote leadership; Brian, wearing grubby clothing to echo Pollution; Wensleydale, whose appetite for a healthy lunch connects him to Famine; Pepper, a spirited girl who shares a taste for red with War.

Alfie Taylor is equally drawn to his character, but doesn't see himself in Wensleydale as Amma does in Pepper. 'Wensleydale likes science and how things work. He's nerdy and kind of in his own world compared to the others, which isn't really me. I'm not especially intelligent,' Alfie offers sadly as if to qualify the point, and then grins at how that comes across. 'But like him I do wear glasses!'

Ilan Galkoff believes he has previous form when it comes to playing a role such as Brian. 'My family say I'm always picked to play the grubby one,' he laughs. 'He's so different to me. I'm like a total neat freak. Brian is also quite immature in some ways. He just sort of hangs around the others.'

Listening to his three young co-stars is the thirteen-year-old who plays the Son of Satan. Sam Taylor Buck is flopped in a chair with his hands on the armrests. Whether or not he's aware of the impression this creates in view of his role, Sam looks like a prince upon his throne before his loyal courtiers. He sports a mop of curly chestnut hair and a steel blue gaze I find a little disconcerting given the character he plays. Happily, he also smiles throughout and sounds endearingly upbeat when discussing the part.

'Well, he's the Antichrist, but because of a mix-up at birth he joins a normal family. So he has this stable background and becomes quite a well-raised child.' Sam speaks as if building towards the punch line to a joke. 'In his nature, Adam is someone who wants to kill everyone and destroy the world, but he's also a peaceful, happy boy.'

So how does a normal, charming and engaging kid from Sheffield approach a character known affectionately in the novel as the Adversary, Destroyer of Kings, Angel of the Bottomless Pit, Great Beast that is called Dragon, Prince of this World, Father of Lies, Spawn of Satan and Father of Darkness? Sam takes the question in his stride.

'I play him as a split personality who phases in and out of being really quite horrible and then being normal,' he says. 'I just have to imagine what it would be like to be this boy who has a voice in his ear telling him to destroy everything. My friends are terrified of the Antichrist, but they really like Adam,' he adds, looking warmly around at the others.

On screen, Sam is clearly comfortable with both sides of his character. It's brought together, as costume designer Claire Anderson sees it, by a quality present in each one. 'Adam is a leader,' she says. 'He's in charge of his gang even before he knows he's the Antichrist. I dressed him in blue because it's strong and fresh and makes him look the most handsome of his counterparts. So he looks familiar and comfortable but with touches of timelessness. He could be a child from the fifties or from today.' There is no doubt that the four young actors consider the experience of working on *Good Omens* as a grand adventure. They're also well aware that sharing the screen with a cast that includes David Tennant, Michael Sheen and Miranda Richardson among many others is a dream come true so early in their careers.

'I've loved seeing so many amazing actors perform in real life,' says Ilan.

'It's been amazing working with the cast,' agrees Sam. 'You learn so much from everything going on around you, including the hundreds of different jobs going on on set.'

The four nominate a wealth of high points in their work on the production, from working with stunt coordinator Cedric Proust on the wires to gaining

Unaware of his stirring powers, and with Anathema's dog-eared *New Aquarian* magazines at hand, Adam's interest in unexplained phenomena gives rise to a host of startling events around the world, from the rise of the Kraken to a close encounter with a UFO.

insight into special and visual effects. When asked to name their greatest challenge, however, Sam, Amma, Ilan and Alfie are in complete agreement, and their response is surprising.

'I'm going to say the ice-cream eating,' says Amma, referring to a halcyon scene in Episode Two that takes place before the gang become aware that their leader is in fact the Son of Satan. 'I'm not a fan, and I don't like vanilla at all, and I got vanilla. We had to do thirty-nines takes of ice cream eating. And twenty-five with ice lollies. And it was just awful. My ice lolly also had vanilla ice cream in it, and I got brain freeze.'

'I got vanilla as well,' says Sam. 'But I prefer chocolate.'

Alfie exchanges a look with him as if they're both still troubled by the memory.

'I had strawberry,' he says. 'I really don't like strawberry.'

All eyes turn to Ilan Galkoff, who admits the flavour wasn't the issue for him. 'I had to take a whole double cone of chocolate ice cream and shove it in my mouth,' he says. 'It was incredibly difficult.'

As all four actors are under the age of sixteen, strict guidelines come into play with regard to both their welfare and schooling. A chaperone accompanies the children throughout the production, who constantly records the time they've spent working to ensure the production complies with UK law. She's also on hand to remind them of one other scene during the shoot that proved to be a steep learning curve, which prompts laughter from them all.

'This is going to sound really bad,' says Ilan. 'But I'm fourteen and can't ride a bike.' With some diplomacy, the chaperone points out that every one of them struggled at first in the saddle.

'I had a retro chopper with a basket on the front which Ollie the dog sat in,' says Sam, referring to the canine that played the role of the Antichrist's reshaped hell-hound. 'Ollie squirmed around whenever we were riding, which made things difficult,' he adds. Then, with a mischievous gleam appearing in his eyes, Sam goes on to mention an incident on the *Good Omens* shoot that proved inconsequential but was subsequently amplified in the British press. 'Ollie is the one that bit David Tennant,' he declares, and gleefully lords over the awkward silence that follows.

When asked about their most challenging moment of the production, all four young actors who play the Them nominated the multiple takes it took to nail the ice-cream-eating scene.

WITCHES AND WITCHFINDERS

In which we return to the origins of the Nice and Accurate Prophecies, and learn not to buy Betamax.

'We burned a witch on Halloween,' says first assistant director Cesco Reidy, about the 31 October shoot. 'I've always wanted to do that.'

Of course, the events in *Good Omens* should come as no surprise to anyone with the gift of foresight. In Terry and Neil's novel, one seventeenth-century visionary predicted the fate of the world with such conviction that she wrote it all down in her book, *The Nice and Accurate Prophecies of Agnes Nutter, Witch*, and duly published to qualify for the complimentary author copy.

In narrative terms, as Neil Gaiman recognized on adapting the book for the screen, the dramatic fate of Nutter and the legacy she left behind could not be treated as a simple flashback. In his mind, the book of prophecies penned by Terry Pratchett's wonderfully witchy and comic creation sets up Aziraphale and Crowley's bid to undermine Armageddon. As a result, the team set out to shoot one of the most explosive scenes of the series in a detailed recreation of a Lancashire village in 1656.

'We went to the Weald and Downland Living Museum, near Chichester in West Sussex,' says the location manager Nick Marshall. A faithful recreation of a seventeenth-century village, found amid a fifty-acre site that houses reconstructions that span a thousand years of English rural life, Nick and the advance scouting party immediately recognized the set-build savings and sense of authenticity to be gained from shooting at the location. 'It was a no-brainer,' he says quite simply, as producer Phil Collinson agrees.

'It's just an incredible park where they rescue historical buildings that are going to be demolished,' he explains. 'So they take them down bit by bit, shift

The Weald and Downland Living Museum in West Sussex provided a faithful recreation of a seventeen-century English village – the perfect setting for a witch burning.

them to the museum site and re-erect them. It meant we didn't have to spend money on a build but the value on screen is incredible. There's a level of detail throughout that allowed us to get everything on camera. There was no need to build a CGI environment. It's all for real.'

Even with what he describes as 'a ready-made set', Cesco Reidy explains that there was still much work to be done before shooting could begin. 'It's a recreation period village, and yet the modern world can still get into camera,' he says. 'With anything related to the public you've got signs saying "toilet", "reception", "this way" – or whatever. Then in a place where you have power and electricity there will be some visible cables, while in the areas that aren't open to the public you'll find modern fencing rather than old-fashioned fencing. There's always something to do,' he says, 'but in the main it's a much better environment for us to work in.'

The scene in Episode Two captures the final events in the life of Agnes Nutter, played with assured and possessed brilliance by Josie Lawrence. We first find her in her cottage, completing a note to her son-in-law, John Device, and daughter, Virtue. She's well aware of the fate about to befall her when Witchfinder Major Pulsifer bursts in (played by Jack Whitehall in a foreshadowing of his central role as modern-day fledgling witchfinder and descendant of his seventeenth-century incarnation, Newt Pulsifer). As well as predicting the fact that she's about to be put to death, Agnes is wise to the witchfinder's own imminent demise and those of the many villagers who will gather around the bonfire to watch her burn at the stake. As for the book Agnes leaves behind, in centuries to come this dusty heirloom will pass into the hands of a young American descendant, Anathema Device. With Armageddon imminent, as cryptically set out in the pages, this student of the supernatural follows her destiny to find herself caught up with Newt in a bid to save the world.

In setting this train of events in motion, production designer Michael Ralph aimed to invest Agnes's cottage with space for the camera to move and meaning for the viewer to absorb on different levels.

'Agnes is burned as a witch because she has a sense of sorcery about her. But the fact is she was just predicting things. So I put in weather instruments

Of the contraptions and gadgets that fill Agnes Nutter's cottage, Michael Ralph says, 'I created all this machinery, but didn't know what it actually did. The point is all these things are connected.'

As well as his role as Newt, Jack Whitehall also appears as his witchfinding ancestor, Thou-Shalt-Not-Commit-Adultery Pulsifer – seen here with Witchfinder Private Maggs (Philip Wright) preparing to deliver Agnes Nutter to her fate.

and a chance for her to play with alchemy. I also gave her a scientific element by creating an old theodolite,' he explains, referring to a surveying instrument with a mounted telescope often used in fields such as meteorology. 'I lined it up with a cross, over a fire in the middle of the room with a pot of water bubbling on it to create steam.' Michael draws breath to consider the picture he's just painted. 'I don't know what any of it does,' he admits with a smile. 'The important thing is that only Agnes could do the things she does with prophecies. She's lined up with the stars, she's part of the Earth, and if she's looking for something only she knows how to find it.'

With Agnes's scene inside the cottage complete, attention turned to the climax of this sequence. Here, with the camera lens pulled back, it fell to first assistant director Cesco Reidy to make sure everything was in place for Douglas Mackinnon to capture the dramatic end to a life foretold.

'We'd prepared 140 acres of grounds,' he says, 'assembled a crowd of supporting actors in period costume and built a huge bonfire for the witch burning.' As Agnes has an explosive surprise up her sleeve as a final act, or in this case hidden within the folds of her skirt, the shoot required the action to finish with an almighty explosion. 'It had to be viewed from above, from the sky looking down,' says Cesco. 'So, once again we found ourselves in a classic *Good Omens* situation in which nothing comes too easily, and we had to work hard to achieve it.'

In order to make sure that Agnes Nutter went out with a visually dramatic bang, key crew members came together to plan the shot in advance. 'My brief was to create a debris explosion which goes up towards the camera and turns the screen black,' explains the special effects supervisor Danny Hargreaves. 'It would give Douglas what he needed to cut to the next scene.'

For such a bold and creative exit from the scene, how did director of photography Gavin Finney feel about positioning a camera over a detonation intended to billow and bloom into its path?

'It had to be real, and not an effect,' he says. 'But Danny is a super-safe person with huge experience. So we suspended the camera from a crane high over the bonfire, with safety glass across the camera to protect the lens.'

As the bonfire intensifies, but before the gunpowder in her nail-packed pockets ignite, Agnes Nutter implores everyone to come closer.
In filming the scene, the crowd were required to throw themselves backwards to mimic the force of the separately filmed blast.

Even with such precautions, Gavin and his team placed a great deal of faith in the *Good Omens* special effects supervisor. How could Danny Hargreaves be sure he wasn't about to obliterate a very expensive piece of kit?

'I want to say I bring out a computer and a calculator,' he confesses, 'but as with anything that you work with day in and day out, you like to think that you know what you're doing. So, I look at the height, I estimate how much black powder I feel we need to use, and then my team nail it.' Danny goes on to outline that a good filmic explosion is made up of two parts, with each requiring a take that can be edited together for the final cut. 'As well as the black debris explosion rising upwards, we staged a second one with more flames at the bottom that spread outwards.'

In bringing the two shots together, Gavin Finney had to ensure that the camera remained completely static in the face of the blast.

'There was also CGI work to be done that would show the crowd on the ground being blown back,' he adds, describing what is in effect a transition from one scene to another that is as exquisitely rendered as the action that unfolds on each side.

Agnes's daughter and son-in-law, Virtue and John Device (Bryony Corrigan and Dan Antopolski), discover her book of prophecies and a letter marked 'In the Evente of My Death'.

AGNES NUTTER

JOSIE LAWRENCE

> 'As the owner of two black cats, I'm sure in olden times I would've been dubbed a witch, too.'

When Josie Lawrence cackles, she does so with the same heart she invests in her *Good Omens* character. Introduced in the novel by Terry Pratchett and Neil Gaiman in her final minutes before being burned at the stake, Agnes Nutter and her prophecies inform every page of the story. In the same way, her spirit spans the TV adaptation, after Agnes leaves behind a book of particular prophecies that are interpreted by a descendant determined to prevent Armageddon, one Anathema Device.

'In many respects, even in a seventeenth-century village atmosphere, I think Agnes was a highly intelligent, modern-day woman.' Josie pauses to further consider her character. 'The men of the village, including the Witchfinder General, they're scared of her because she knows everything in advance. She was probably like a lot of women of that period,' she suggests. 'Someone great with herbs, and who could heal people if they were sick, but because she's a woman, and not behaving as a "normal" woman, therefore she must be a witch. Agnes is smart but with magical qualities,' she offers instead. 'That's how I aim to play her.'

Unlike many of her cast members, coming to the story via the script or the novel, Josie Lawrence had already formed a connection with Agnes Nutter in a different medium.

'I played her in the radio series,' she says, referring to the 2014 BBC radio adaptation of *Good Omens*. 'That's how it all began, and when I decided I adored her. There's a warmth to Agnes. An eccentric kind of warmth. I also think she'd make a fun dinner guest!' Josie is impressive in the screen version of the part she made her own on the radio. She'll also be instantly recognizable to fans of the audio version from the moment she delivers her first line. 'The voice is the same here,' says the actor and comedian with the distinctive West Midlands accent. 'It's a cross between my own and one that suggests she could've come from anywhere.'

A familiar face in the world of comedy, Josie Lawrence has also worked extensively in theatre, television and radio, as well as appearing in several films. In *Good Omens*, Josie calls upon her range and versatility as an actor to unleash a formidable inner spirit in her final act.

'Agnes is an immensely brave and powerful woman,' she says. 'She's preparing for her death when we meet her, which she sorts out in quite an unusual way. It's very practical in the note she leaves for the milkman, saying that she doesn't want any more milk and giving her love to his wife. So it makes me think that she was quite loved by some of the women in the village but not by the men.' Josie concedes that in loading her skirt pockets with gunpowder and nails, Agnes Nutter takes out both male and female villagers who have gathered to watch her burn. 'Well, perhaps she told some of the good 'uns to stay at home!' she laughs.

Josie is equally struck by the particular way in which her character predicts the end of the world. 'Terry and Neil have created this prophetess who sees the future, but often only in an intimate family way and how it affects the people she loves,' she explains. 'Agnes's predictions are precise and also very funny. So, for the day of the JFK assassinations, which she doesn't mention, she warns that a house will fall down in King's Lynn. I think my favourite is "Do Notte Buye Betamacks",' adds Josie. 'I also love that the book of her prophecies never sold, because it was too accurate. But she has it published for the free copy, and then passes it down until it gets to this wonderful strong descendant.'

Josie's passion for the story is evident, as is her admiration for the character who takes Agnes Nutter's book to heart.

'Anathema Device is a modern-day role model. She's a true kind of feminist; her own woman,' she says, speaking of the character we first meet as a little girl in a Californian beachfront condo as her mother prepares her for a quest foretold in Agnes's prophecies. The family have made their millions by cracking

Claire Anderson was very careful to be true to the period in her designs for Agnes Nutter's seventeenth-century costume.

Agnes's cryptic prediction that in 1980 Apple would be a company worth investing in. The fact that a passage in the book concerning Armageddon mentions Anathema by name leaves us in no doubt that her life – and future love interest – has been mapped out before her. It takes a strong-minded girl to answer such a calling, and this is where her focus and resolve is first forged.

Having drawn on her experience with the radio adaptation to summon the spirit of Agnes Nutter, Josie sought to make sure she had the same visual impact. The most immediate challenge, she explains, came down to the fact that she was appearing in theatre as *Good Omens* preparations got underway.

'I was performing in *Mother Courage* in London at the time,' she says, 'and so costume and make-up came to my rehearsal rooms. They wanted Agnes to wear a kind of puritanical hat, but I didn't see her as a hat girl, so we went with loads of hair. I had two wigs, one on top of the other, a particular dress made from very thick fibre and a low-cut tunic. She's very much a Hammer Horror heroine, I think.'

Josie Lawrence speaks highly of Douglas Mackinnon's skill as a director in adapting *Good Omens* for the screen. 'It looks magnificent, and has everything in it,' she says. 'There are moving moments, and it's incredibly witty and funny. Also, I love the idea of two beings having lived for years and years with each other, grown close and got to rather like humanity. Nothing is completely black and white,' she reasons when asked if the story can teach us anything. 'Which is why Agnes isn't completely a witch. She's a woman, and the story is about humanity and how we deal with each other.'

Having worked with Neil Gaiman on the *Good Omens* radio adaptation, Josie regards this latest incarnation to have been another opportunity for her to spend more time with him. 'Neil is such a wonderful human being,' she says. 'He gets on very well with Douglas, and has a warmth about him that gives you a good feeling about the project. You feel that you're joining him in creating something unique, and Neil has got this thing about creating. I admire people who do that. They're constantly living in a world in which they can see things within it differently to the way other human beings can. For me,' Josie Lawrence concludes, 'that was what made it so special about meeting him and being in it.'

AGNES NUTTER: Come close until the fire near scorch ye, for I charge ye that all must see how the last true witch in England dies.

Filming at the Weald and Downland Living Museum in West Sussex took place over two days in October 2017. While her character goes out with a bang, Josie Lawrence was only required to be tied to the stake *before* the flames started rising high.

A PERFECT VILLAGE

In which the cast and crew set out to film scenes of serenity and sorcery in a real village, without trampling on the grass.

'It's a beautiful village. Quintessentially English. It couldn't get more perfect.'

As director of photography, Gavin Finney has a sharp eye for the right location. He's effectively looking through the camera lens at all times, and able to spot problems and possibilities in the blink of an eye. In the adaptation of *Good Omens*, the heart of the action takes place in and around a fictional village that has to go beyond being idyllic. In Terry Pratchett and Neil Gaiman's world, Tadfield is the home of Mr and Mrs Young, and their son, Adam. Unaware of his calling as the Antichrist, this happy boy from loving parents (played with a delightful sense of domesticity by Daniel Mays and Sian Brooke) enjoys an upbringing defined by unbroken summers and crisp, snowy winters. It isn't just his unwitting influence on the weather that's contributed to this bubble of beauty and tranquillity. 'If Turner and Landseer had met Samuel Palmer in a pub and worked it all out,' begins our introduction to Tadfield and the surrounding landscape in the novel itself, 'and then got Stubbs to do the horses, it couldn't have been better.'

On paper, we all have our own concept of perfection. On screen, which leaves little to the imagination, it fell to one man to serve up a village we return to throughout the series that Gavin and his camera could explore to the full.

'It's the heartbeat of the world,' begins Nick Marshall, *Good Omens*' location manager, on describing his search for the ideal village in the pre-production stage. 'As soon as I got the script, I read it in full and then broke it down into locations,' he says, and points out how the list ranged from major London landmarks like St James's Park, the Ritz and Berkeley Square to places that need not be recognizable but fitted the scene, such as the graveyard where

Location manager Nick Marshall whittled down a list of quintessentially English villages to one that will now be known by *Good Omens* fans as a picture-perfect Tadfield.

Hastur and Ligur hand over the Antichrist child to Crowley and the cafe where our demon meets his 'human operative', Shadwell.

'Looking at the list allowed me to absorb the information and let it sink in,' Nick continues. 'In doing so, it struck me that lots of scenes take place in and around Tadfield. There's Adam's house, Anathema's cottage, Tadfield Airbase and Tadfield Manor, as well as action in various lanes and woodland. So the next step for me was to identify a village that would also mean we wouldn't have to travel far to cover everything.'

In his role as a film and television location manager Nick Marshall spends much of his time cultivating a database of places of note. He's constantly on the lookout for locations to shoot film and television productions. In his search for a suitable Tadfield, Nick says that one village in particular immediately sprang to his mind.

'Hambleden came to me automatically,' he says of the picturesque village near Henley-on-Thames, forty miles west of London, and explains that it is one of a shortlist of five that he submitted to Douglas and his team for consideration. 'It offered everything in terms of appearance, but also meant we could reach other key locations easily like RAF Upper Heyford and Bulstrode Park,' he adds, referring to the sites that were used for Tadfield Airbase and the convent-cum-conference centre respectively.

'Tadfield is meant to be a chocolate-box village, and Hambleden is exactly that,' agrees producer Phil Collinson. 'The buildings have thatched roofs; there's a village green and a red telephone box. But you have to be very careful,' he cautions. 'You don't want to be annoying everyone.'

Phil is well versed in the importance of treating locations where people live and work with the utmost respect. It's a view shared with his *Good Omens* colleagues, who were mindful of the scale of the production.

'It was a takeover,' says first assistant director Cesco Reidy, 'and so we had a responsibility to the village. You cannot approach a location like this with any degree of ownership or entitlement. That would be a terrible error. One has to be diplomatic and listen. It means we had to think ahead about what we want to do and how that might inconvenience people.'

Phil Collinson considers the key factor to maintaining good relations is to know what's required from the location in advance of the arrival of what can seem like the movie-making equivalent of a fairground.

'You have to be considerate and careful and disciplined about where you want to film, and then stick to the plan in order to get the best out of it,' he advises. 'Often locals are chuffed to be in it, but the reality can be awful for them if cast and crew come and trample on their daffodils or walk on their nice new carpet. So a big part of what we do is manage the locations and be respectful of them and the people there.'

In preparing to film in Hambleden, Nick Marshall assumed responsibility for forging a working relationship between the production and the locals.

'It's about managing expectations,' he says. 'So I went in and liaised with everyone. From the parish council to estates and tenants, private owners, shops, pubs, the staff, refuse workers, delivery people, the garage and the church, I made friends with everyone.' During this process, Nick outlined what the production was about and their plans for shooting in and around the area, not just in person but on paper. 'I wrote a letter to everybody in the village, and

With filming taking place around Hambleden, the *Good Omens* cast and crew worked closely with the village community to minimise disruption.

Actor Ilan Galkoff
takes time out on
his bike in between
takes during the
Hambleden shoot. By
their own admission,
and much to the
surprise of the
crew, none of the
Them found riding
to be easy.

hand delivered each one,' he explains. 'It's beneficial to the production, and I enjoy the experience. It's a positive exercise. Together with my team, I aim to be a nice guy. A human face for the shoot. Someone positive and relatable.'

It would be easy, he says, for him to paint a favourable picture of the process, but in Nick's view that would simply be creating potential problems at a critical time. 'A shoot the size of *Good Omens* is a massive disruption,' he says. 'As it involves road closures, people deserve to know. There's no point pretending to be a small production, or saying we're only filming for two days if we plan to be there for five. If anything, I suggest we'll be shooting for longer than planned. That way, people are pleasantly surprised.'

With the groundwork laid by Nick, the *Good Omens* cast and crew arrived to a warm reception.

'Everyone was very open to us,' says script supervisor Jemima Thomas. 'This is a bigger machine than most productions. We bring in a lot of equipment, and use everything all the time, so all credit to Nick for preparing the way.'

In view of Nick's efforts, and mindful that a good relationship with the people of the village would enable them to make the most of the setting, both cast and crew of *Good Omens* set to work with a heightened awareness of their surroundings. Cesco Reidy believes this always comes down to a phrase at the heart of his work: plan the shoot and shoot the plan.

'If we had agreed to stop traffic for two minutes at a time then we had to adhere to that,' he says. 'We can't go stopping it for ten minutes as that would've driven people mad. We're also constantly looking out from set to the horizon to see if someone is approaching or heading for a shop on camera. It's fine to approach and ask if they'd mind staying out of shot but you have to be respectful. A couple of times someone would say something like, "I'm coming through here with a lorry later to pick up some stuff, will you be filming?" And we always did our level best to accommodate them so their lives aren't interrupted.'

Like Jemima Thomas, Cesco agrees that the advance work of the location manager is central to the success of a shoot in a living environment. 'We were there for a couple of weeks,' he says of an intense period of filming scenes inside and outside of the Youngs' house and Anathema's cottage as well as with the Them across the village streets. 'We even went back for one or two days later on, and the people of Hambleden were lovely. Absolutely delightful. Not a single person gave us any cause for concern. It worked very well, and that was down to Nick and his team. People are getting on with their lives here. They're doing the shopping, taking the kids to school and getting from A to B. It's on my mind throughout the shoot and a matter of constant management. As for the work, as soon as the camera rolls then *Good Omens* kicks in again. We've got bikers coming through the high street, kids to care for and a storm sequence involving hurricane-level wind machines. In that situation, within a village environment, I'm like a magician spinning plates. It's as if I'm constantly trying to get ahead of them.'

With the freedom to make the most of Hambledon as a location, director of photography Gavin Finney aimed high.

'We brought in the drone for overhead shots,' he explains. 'We used track, dolly and technocrane so that we can quickly establish that we're in a beautiful English village, and then we drop down or zoom into the action.'

On the ground, overseeing a dedicated team, special effect supervisor Danny Hargreaves worked to create a visually compelling atmosphere to complement the action.

'I like to put a bit of movement into a location,' Danny says. 'In both interior and exterior settings, a little smoke or fog can be interesting to the eye. We might be filming in woods or a shop, but putting something into the shot stops it from being static.'

Danny points out the obvious challenges of working outside with fog and smoke, and again stresses the important of bringing the people of Hambleden onside. 'You can't contain smoke cover, but we were pretty much able to do what we wanted,' he says.

Such creative freedom even extended to Danny during a scene in Episode Four when a pre-apocalyptic storm unleashes a tornado over Tadfield and forces Newt and Anathema to take refuge under the bed inside her cottage. 'We brought in the rain and trailer-mounted wind machines,' he says, 'and then Douglas asked for a tree to fly through the back of the shot just as Jack Whitehall is being sucked into the air. I had to think about this for a while,' he

Acclaimed British actor Bill Paterson makes an appearance in *Good Omens* as Tadfield's village busybody, R. P. Tyler...

laughs. 'Basically, we found a large branch that looked tree-like, turned the air mover up to max and launched it across the shot. See if you can spot it!'

In terms of making full use of the location, Gavin Finney recalls shooting a scene with the Them walking through Tadfield. 'We wanted to give the village a bucolic feel here,' he begins. 'So we arranged to have fifty sheep heading down a path. Douglas felt that sheep were English, and in fact that part of the world around Hambleden made its money through sheep. Even if just in the background, Douglas likes that attention to detail.' While the director had full control of the picture, it seems the sheep had other ideas.

'They were meant to be coming in behind us, and then follow a path that extended from the road we were walking down,' explains Sam Taylor Buck, who plays Adam Young and is well aware that he's set to tell a tale about filming with children and animals. 'Instead, they came out and ran towards us like a massive fluffy tide. We scattered, and people were trying to block them from getting past. It was chaos! I had Ollie the dog in the basket on the front of my bike. He tried to jump out and chase them, but his lead was tied to the basket and that held him back. So then *he* had to be rescued as well!'

... seen here on patrol with his sausage dog, Shutzi.

Filming with children and animals. In a bid to make one village scene with the Them quintessentially English, Douglas populated the lane with a herd of sheep... which subsequently bolted mid-shoot.

As well as being home to Adam and the Them, Tadfield is also the location for Jasmine Cottage, which is where we find new resident and Agnes Nutter descendant Anathema Device. In the story, she's arrived in Tadfield from America with maps and contraptions, determined to read between the lines of her ancestor's prophecies and prevent the end of the world. Hambleden boasted a picturesque cottage and garden that would serve perfectly as Anathema's rented home. The kitchen and hallway downstairs were suitably dressed by production designer Michael Ralph and his team.

Producer Phil Collinson explains why they decided that the scenes taking place on the next floor would be better hosted elsewhere.

'Bedrooms are notoriously difficult spaces to film in,' he says. 'They're upstairs, which makes it difficult to get equipment up and down, and tend to be cramped for a cast and crew.' As a result, when Anathema and Newt take things to the next level, the cottage shoot moved from a real-life location in Buckinghamshire to a set built in Cape Town, South Africa.

Like so many things in the world of *Good Omens*, everything is quite literally not as it seems.

Anathema arrives at Jasmine Cottage, her home in a village that Terry and Neil describe in the novel as one that could have been cobbled together by Old Masters.

ANATHEMA DEVICE

ADRIA ARJONA

'I am a disaster in the head. A mess. I focus on about twenty different things at the same time, and Anathema is the opposite of that.'

Adria Arjona is an expressive woman. She illustrates a great deal of what she says with her hands, as if to shape her words, which she puts down to her Latin-American blood. The American actress of Puerto Rican and Guatemalan descent might be far from home, but she's in her element playing the young descendant of Agnes Nutter. As a practical occultist, Anathema is on a mission to decipher her ancestor's prophecies and ultimately save the world. Through Adria's eyes, however, she's more than just a witch.

'I see auras,' she says, speaking to me about her character while waiting to be called to set at West London Film Studios. Later, with cameras rolling, I'll watch Aziraphale dust down Anathema after Crowley accidentally knocks her from her bicycle in the Bentley. In this scene, Adria delivers an excellent performance as a young woman who relies on her instincts to guide and protect her. 'I can identify if someone can be trusted, or if they're a good person, but these are inherited powers,' Adria points out, and outlines how it guides Anathema's calling. 'You see me as a little kid, studying the *Nice and Accurate Prophecies*, and get the feeling that this girl lives and breathes it. She's smart, but only from this book. Good social skills aren't that important to her. She's just focused on this one specific job,' says Adria of Anathema's quest to prevent the apocalypse, 'and wants to get it done well to make her family proud. So she leaves everything behind to get it done. She knows Armageddon is happening. She just doesn't know where, when, how or who is involved. She has to figure that out.'

In discussing how she came to the role, Adria Arjona describes an approach she applies to all film and television projects. 'When I receive a script, I tend to tear out the first page,' she says. 'This way, I won't know who wrote it, the producer or the director. If I'm told Robert de Niro is starring in it then the script could be terrible but I'm going to say that I love it, y'know? So, I read the script without that knowledge, and if I'm drawn to it and I think it's a challenge, and I can imagine me doing it, then I'll go ahead. And *Good Omens* is a strong script!' she declares happily. 'It was different to anything I'd done before. The accent is different. The rhythm is different. *Everything* is different! It's also based on a novel by Terry Pratchett and Neil Gaiman, with Neil as showrunner, and I don't always get that lucky! Having him here is brilliant,' she says. 'It's a gift, and I want to do it justice.'

Watching Adria Arjona's interpretation of Anathema, there's no doubt that she admires her character's drive and spirit. She agrees with Josie Lawrence, who plays her ancestor, Agnes Nutter, that these are women bonded by a shared quality. 'She's a strong woman,' says Adria. 'It's inherited and in her veins. Anathema knows her purpose. I also think a great deal of confidence comes from someone who knows how to use that as a strength. That's the journey Anathema goes through. From the second she leaves her house in LA for England, she goes out of her comfort zone. She's independent, living in a beautiful cottage, and all these things start sparking off in her. We see her discover herself, and even who she really is without the book.'

Making her name in HBO's *True Detective*, Adria Arjona has a flair for inhabiting her roles with great poise, heart and soul. Does this come from an inner confidence?

'No actor is confident,' she counters. 'We just pretend! I come from a very secure family base, and that's something Anathema has. Other than that, I've had to create a lot of it, especially as so much of it is magical. She talks about ley lines, for example, and so I've had to do my own investigations and spend some time with people who understand these things.'

Candidly, Adria explains that it was a line of enquiry that didn't bear as much fruit as she had hoped. 'I didn't feel I could act based on intellectual research alone. I didn't have her somehow.' Instead, calling upon the experience of someone close to her, Adria positioned her character as an individual

Character sketches by Claire Anderson for Anathema Device as a girl obsessed by the prophecies of her ancestor, Agnes Nutter, and as the young woman who follows her destiny to Tadfield.

approaching something bordering a religious conversion. 'I have a friend who wants to become a nun,' she explains. 'Seeing her go through this process, and witnessing her be so passionately focused on one thing and forgetting about everything else, was an inspiration to me. In the same way, I saw Anathema as having no choice about whether to believe the book. It's more like a conviction. She's been brought up knowing she had to believe in it in order to save the world. So, there's a bigger picture here,' she adds, and explains that it fits in with her view that *Good Omens* is a satire on the concept of religion. 'This is someone who is stuck to one book. She cannot see anything around it. And I also love her selflessness. Anathema gives up everything, her life essentially, to save everyone else.'

In understanding her character, and inhabiting the role so readily, Adria claims the key moment came when she literally climbed into Anathema's shoes.

'I just got it!' she declares, gazing down at where her character's stockings meet her pointed boots. 'I tried them on and something in my body changed.'

If Dorothy from the *Wizard of Oz* could channel Glinda the Good Witch of the South, the outcome would look a lot like Adria Arjona's Anathema Device.

ANATHEMA: I was hoping he wouldn't come. If he didn't turn up... maybe none of it was real. But if he's here, then the Beast is real.

'She's elegant and beautiful but she's a witch,' says *Good Omens*' costume designer Claire Anderson, who worked with Adria on creating the look. Rather than go full witch, however, Claire took a more subtle approach in which symbolism carried most weight. 'A good costume shouldn't dominate the scene, but it does lead the character,' she explains. 'So I focused on elements of witchiness and that included Anathema's bicycle. Her coat is based on a late Victorian cycling coat. It's cinched, which gives her an old-fashioned feminine shape, and worn with a full skirt. That made her slightly out of time and nearly normal but not quite. I also wanted her to be dark, but not black like Crowley, along with some colour that would grow from young Anathema to the woman she becomes.'

Adria is discussing her role with her dark hair pinned back. A contribution from hair and make-up designer Nosh Oldham, it's another visual reference to the journey her character undertakes as her quest increasingly possesses her.

'My hair goes down as I become more witchy, more myself and less in control. It represents a sense of freedom as it falls,' says Adria, and goes on to credit

In the wake of an odd little road accident en route to Tadfield, Newt is rescued by the Them and lays eyes on Anathema for the first time.

both Nosh and Claire for their work in helping her to bring her character into focus. 'Filmmaking is a complete collaboration,' she says. 'Little things spark between us and it becomes a middle ground where everyone feels comfortable and in love with the look.'

In relocating to Tadfield, the very model of a conservative English village, Adria's young Californian occultist naturally stands out to the locals. In Episode Three she's stopped in the street by Neighbourhood Watch busybody, R. P. Tyler (played by Scottish television actor Bill Paterson), and also runs into the Them as they play a game called the British Inquisition. 'I love working with the kids,' she says of her young co-stars. 'Seeing how they embody this whole process has been incredible.' Adria speaks highly of every member of the *Good Omens* cast and crew, but reserves special praise for Jack Whitehall, the actor who shares the most screen time with her.

'Anathema isn't drawn to Newt, but it's in the prophecy. She knows he's coming, and she's prepared, and then she gets Jack!' she laughs. 'So, it's OK when she sees him. She sees his vulnerability and sensitivity.'

An apprentice witchfinder, Newt is an introverted character who arrives in Tadfield to investigate strange weather patterns that might suggest an occult presence. But with time ticking towards the Apocalypse, and Adam's daydreams impacting on the world around him, strange events are taking shape. On his way to the village, Newt encounters bumbling aliens from a flying saucer before crashing his car when a pair of tunnelling monks from Tibet surface in the road. Rescued by the Them, the shaken Newt finds himself in Anathema's care. What impact does Adria feel that her character has on him?

'She's always pushing him,' she says. 'She's constantly pushing his boundaries, and also tearing him down because of his lack of confidence. She's definitely a lot stronger than Newt, and towards the end that helps him to become stronger.' Adria spreads her hands. 'That's when she looks at him and thinks, "You're kind of cute."'

At one point in *Good Omens*, Anathema and Jack Whitehall's Newt are thrown together not just emotionally but into the heart of a storm. Adria considers it to be a high point of the shoot in every way.

With the Nice and Accurate Prophecies committed to index cards, Anathema strives to get ahead of Armageddon even after the book goes missing.

ANATHEMA: My family has been figuring our Agnes's prophecies for four hundred years now. You could say we're professional descendents.

'We had to do this shot where we're lifted into the air on rigs, with wind and rain and leaves flying at us.' It's a demanding scene, in which Anathema fights to save Newt from being sucked into the maelstrom and showcases Adria's physical range.

Adria's passion for all aspects of acting is matched by her interest in the craft behind the camera. She talks of her ambition to direct, and reveals how Douglas Mackinnon allowed her to shadow him on the *Good Omens* production, from scouting locations to the shoot itself.

'I'll do my scene and then stay watching,' she says. 'I also go in when I'm not working and then observe how he frames shots. Douglas is very practical as a director and extremely specific as a storyteller.'

Adria Arjona's enthusiasm for her role, her craft and the world around her is dizzying. She's upbeat and energetic with a spirit of enquiry and a hunger to learn. Reflecting on her experience with *Good Omens*, she feels that her character has been a grounding influence.

'I've had to tune into Anathema and see how she does things,' she says. 'Thanks to her, I've become a bit more organized.'

While most of the key characters were arriving at the airbase through the front gate, Anathema and Newt followed the prophecies and slipped in through the perimeter fence at the back and headed to the communications centre.

NEWT: Think of it this way. Do you want to be a descendant all of your life?

All good things must come to an end. Anathema is persuaded by Newt to perform a ritual burning of their own.

NEWTON PULSIFER

JACK WHITEHALL

'I want Newt to be one of those people who is constantly apologizing for his very existence.'

In his character outline for the rudderless young man who finds his calling in a curious modern-day Witchfinder Army, Neil Gaiman describes Newton Pulsifer (or Newt) as 'really smart, really sensible and really unlucky'. Jack Whitehall, the stand-up comedian and actor, rests his head back in the car seat and considers what marked him out for the role.

'I'm probably not that smart or as sensible,' he decides after a moment, 'but I am extremely unlucky. So that bit isn't much of a departure from the real me.'

Certainly Jack can't be referring to his professional life, which has seen him sell out arena tours with his solo shows and star in TV series such as *Fresh Meat* and *Bad Education*, which he co-wrote. He's a familiar face on stage and on screen, but in *Good Omens* it takes a moment to recognize Jack Whitehall without his trademark stubble. It isn't the first time he's been clean-shaven for a role, having starred in the TV adaptation of Evelyn Waugh's *Decline and Fall*, and yet his transformation here into a reluctant modern-day witchfinder is striking.

In Newton Pulsifer, Jack has also nailed the part of a reserved, awkward and inward-looking geek – a departure from his usual gregarious roles – who finds his confidence and spreads his wings in doing his bit to save the world from Armageddon. Having just finished filming for the day, on location at the south London suburban house that serves as his character's home in Dorking, Jack stretches his long legs in the back of the car taking us across the capital at dusk and reflects on his *Good Omens* experience.

'I took on the role because I'm a huge fan of the book,' he tells me. 'I read it at school and loved the tone. It's my kind of comedy, and so when I heard about

Mother knows best. As Newt prepares to leave his Dorking home, and by extension save the world, Mrs Pulsifer (Nicola Harrison) sends him on his way with a nice packed lunch.

the project I was really keen to be involved. I was so delighted when they asked me to play Newt, but I was seeking it out a bit,' he admits.

Jack explains that it was only after he landed the role that he had the opportunity to read the script.

'It was so different,' he says, describing his admiration for Neil's adaptation of the original novel. 'Famously, the book was supposed to be unfilmable, and so to get it into six hours with such world-building and ambition is quite a task. He's done a great job.'

As a fan of *Good Omens* as a schoolboy, Jack Whitehall was well aware of one notable absence from the moment he sat down at the table read-through.

'It's always a high-pressure start to a project,' he explains. 'This time we were told it was Terry Pratchett's dying wish that we made it, and that we shouldn't mess it up, and from that moment on it felt like he was with us. Of course, we all wanted to make it good and make it right for Terry, and Neil is always pointing out lines or scenes that Terry wrote, some of which involve Newt so that made it pretty special.'

In the story, as Jack outlines, we find Newt at a low ebb early in life.

Costume designer Claire Anderson explains that she chose mustard for Newt because she finds it 'a good colour for geeky people'. She also used coat badges and epaulets to link the reluctant, modern-day witchfinder with his seventeenth-century ancestor.

'He's a sort of hapless computer engineer who is slightly cursed when it comes to technology. Basically, everything he touches goes wrong. So he's out of a job, a bit of a lost soul, and then he discovers Shadwell, which is how we first meet him.'

Newt's encounter with the Witchfinder Sergeant, and his recruitment as a Witchfinder Private, is foreshadowed in the adaptation with a delightful appearance by Jack as the seventeenth-century witchfinder who summons Agnes Nutter to the stake. Watching Thou-Shalt-Not-Commit-Adultery Pulsifer in action, resplendent in period costume and a striking hat, it's clear that Jack is relishing his role.

When Jack talks about Newt's mindset and motivation, it's evident he's explored the character in full.

'As is always the way, you find similarities that you recognize in yourself that you try to bring into the role,' explains Jack. 'In this case, I can be socially awkward sometimes. Also, as a teenager, an inability to speak to women was *definitely* me, and so I recognize those aspects and build on them. I want Newt to be one of those people who is constantly apologizing for his very existence.'

Jack Whitehall understands that working on a screen adaptation of a novel such as *Good Omens* provides him with plenty of source material.

'I have a script and the novel, and access to the director and a writer who is very helpful and smart if I want to interrogate something,' he says. 'So, there are avenues to learn more about my character. For example, there's a line that I found really useful about how if Newt ran into a phone booth to change he'd come out as Clark Kent. That really gives me some insight into the type of person he is. He also wears odd-coloured socks, which I asked for as it's in the novel. It's a small detail, but just helps to build a character from the ground up.'

As a comedian used to improvizing on stage, did Jack consider taking things in his own direction? 'I stuck to the script religiously as it's so good,' he says, before praising the light and shade within it. 'There are a few moving pieces because of the density of the story, but the great thing is we have the voice of God to get us out of trouble,' he adds, referring to Frances McDormand's stellar voiceover.

With the help of costume designer Claire Anderson, Newt's clothing went on to provide Jack with another building block in the creation of his character.

'His clothes and haircut are drab,' he says. 'Physicality is really important, I think, as Newt is so uncomfortable in his own skin.' In the same breath, Jack lights up at the mention of his witchfinder's jacket. 'It's Newt's superhero cape,' he says. 'It has a pronounced collar, which is a subtle nod to the look of the puritanical witchfinders like the one I play in the witch-burning scene. There are lots of associations like that, which is down to Claire doing such a great job.' To complete Newt's physical appearance, hair and make-up designer Nosh Oldham purposely applied a light touch.

'He looks younger without the stubble,' she says of Jack, 'and that just seemed right. We also cut his hair to look a bit dishevelled, and that was it. Sometimes, the art is just to leave it be,' she adds. 'Don't overegg the pudding, as my mother used to say.'

If Newt is a young man who wants to believe in something, Jack Whitehall considers why his character should find the answer in witchfinding and not party politics, football or the environment.

NEWT: Oh, come on! The world isn't really going to end today.

Anathema and Newt's growing relationship is explored in full throughout *Good Omens*, with the added twist that Agnes Nutter saw it all coming centuries earlier. While Newt confesses that he's not really a witchfinder, Anathema tells him 'I'm really a witch'. In short, they're a perfect match.

'It's a bolt from the blue for Newt when he comes across Shadwell,' he says, referring to the dishevelled but engagingly passionate and self-styled Witchfinder Sergeant played to glorious effect by Michael McKean. 'Somehow, Newt is seduced by the madness. Shadwell sweeps him up and at that moment in his life he's willing to be swept along. He wants to find something, and have some purpose, and Shadwell just happens to be that purpose. But you get the sense that Newt doesn't really believe in witchfinding,' he points out. 'It's just something to keep him out of the house and make him feel useful.'

In addition to finding his calling, we see Newton Pulsifer's character deepen and develop over the course of the story. From his suburban beginning in a terraced house in Dorking, complete with model aircraft hanging from his bedroom ceiling, Newt embarks upon a journey that will see him in a passionate clinch with a beautiful young visionary in the face of an apocalyptic storm raging outside.

'It's a big development from boy to man,' Jack agrees. 'Newt is painfully shy at the beginning, and very nervous, and then slowly becomes better at asserting

NEWT: Easy. If I actually wanted to get these computers working better, I'd just click on this disk defragmenter and, and...

himself and getting his opinion across. On his way to stopping the end of the world he becomes quite sarcastic,' Jack adds. 'That's been fun to play with as I've got somewhere to go with him. As for Anathema,' he says of Agnes Nutter's descendant, played by Adria Arjona, 'she deflowers him physically but then takes him under her wing. She's a confident and alluring lady, and Newt has never been kissed, so he's quite heavily punching above his weight. But then Anathema challenges and excites him.'

Without doubt, Jack Whitehall is a household name as a comedian, and earning notable acclaim as an actor, but how does it feel working alongside people he considers to be icons of stage and screen?

'Michael McKean is a hero of mine,' he says straight away. 'I love his stuff like *Spinal Tap* and *Best in Show*. His collaborations with Christopher Guest are some of my favourite films, so to work with him has been a dream come true. Then Michael Sheen and David Tennant are so good, and so lovely, and it's such a privilege to be part of this ensemble. It's given me the chance to

Jack Whitehall compares himself to Newt in that he considers himself to be a technophobe. 'Although Newt is keen to learn,' he says. 'Unlike me.'

see their process,' he continues. 'Things like the kind of questions they ask the director. It's been so useful to be on set with people like this.'

As for working with Douglas Mackinnon, Jack considers *Good Omens* to be in the best possible hands with him.

'He really knows what he's doing,' he says. 'Douglas does great dramatic work, but also has a very good understanding of comedy. He makes everything look fantastic, and he's very collaborative.' As an example, Jack mentions the challenge of shooting to a schedule that's out of narrative order. 'It can be hard to track the journey of the character and pitch it with the right tone every day,' he says. 'That's when I rely on someone like Douglas. He can spot these things and keep everything true.' Jack is also mindful that Douglas is effectively the skipper of a vast ship. 'It's a big-scale production,' he agrees. 'Bigger than anything I've been involved in before, with huge sets and an incredible artistic vision, and every toy at their disposal. It's great to be part of something so exciting and so distinct. Jack glances out of the car window as night falls over London. 'I feel a sign of a good project is when it genuinely isn't like anything I've seen on TV before.'

Newt opens the door of Jasmine Cottage to solicitor Giles Baddicombe (Sanjeev Bhaskar) and a package entrusted to his firm for three hundred years. While the package is a surprise to Newt and Anathema, the further prophecies it contains have been penned by Agnes Nutter – and set out the future for them both.

MR AND MRS YOUNG

DANIEL MAYS – *ARTHUR*
SIAN BROOKE – *DEIRDRE*

> Daniel Mays considers himself to be blessed in two ways. Not only is he playing in a major television series he considers to be 'phenomenal', he's acting alongside Sian Brooke whom he regards with great affection.

'We appeared together in my first ever play at the Royal Court Theatre in 2001,' he says. 'This is only our second time working with each other, and so it's been a joy to have her as my on-screen wife. We've had lots of catching up to do on set.'

As Deidre and Arthur, or Mr and Mrs Young, Daniel Mays and Sian Brooke play the unwitting targets of the infernal baby swap that sees them raise a son, Adam, little knowing that on reaching his eleventh birthday he's destined to oversee the world's destruction. While Adam is unaware of his destiny, and his powers to influence the world around him, it's a testament to his parents that his grounded upbringing in Tadfield has given rise to an idyllic childhood. It's a role that clearly delights them both.

'There's an element of stiff upper lip about them,' Daniel explains. 'Arthur is quite strait-laced, and I guess that personality fits in quite well with him providing a stable environment for Adam. Obviously there's a lot more going on with his son than growing pains,' he says about Adam's awakening as the Antichrist, 'and that scenario lends itself to high comedy.'

'They are your typical English parents,' agrees Sian. 'They're the norm that threads through the piece. We represent stability, the epitome of goodness. Compared to some of the mad, evil characters I've done, it was really enjoyable to play Deirdre in this beast of a show.'

A familiar face in *Sherlock* as sibling Eurus Holmes, Sian Brooke has also appeared in the BBC's *Doctor Foster* and starred in *Moorside* with Sheridan

MRS YOUNG: He's down in Hogback Wood, playing with his friends. I told him to be home by teatime.

Shot on location in Hambleden, Mr and Mrs Young's home embodies their role as parents who provide stability for their son to grow... into the Antichrist chid.

Smith. How did she feel entering such a new world for her created by two masters of fantasy and imaginative fiction?

'I went to the reading and realized this was going to be something very special,' she says, 'and not just because it's loved by so many people. The genius of Neil and Terry's writing is that the characters are so fully formed immediately. You get them, and fans of the novel already love them. It's very exciting, and Neil has been so generous with his support. He has such a clear vision and a true love for the story, and also a great sense of fun. He's open to suggestions and trying things out, but ultimately his vision is strong, which is much needed as an actor. He's a bit like a bible,' suggests Sian. 'He knows everything and how things should be.'

From Mike Leigh films such as *All or Nothing* and *Vera Drake* to TV action dramas, including a notable performance as Firearms Officer Danny Waldron in *Line of Duty*, as well as numerous theatre productions, Daniel Mays has shown himself to be an actor of great range and versatility. How did it feel joining *Good Omens* to play someone intended to be so ordinary? Like so

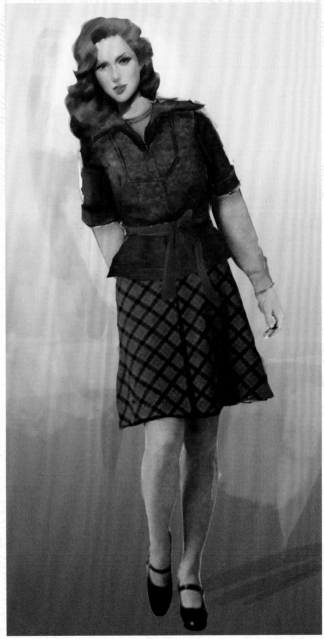

Claire Anderson aimed to create a timeless, comforting appearance for Mr and Mrs Young inspired by the familiarity of the clothes her parents' friends wore when she was growing up.

many of the roles that made his name, Daniel sees Arthur Young as a man whose resilience ultimately defines him.

'It's just a lovely storyline,' he says. 'It's about that human instinct to care for your child no matter how off the rails they are. So Arthur Young raises his child as best he can and fights his corner to the bitter end. There's a heroic quality that comes through in him,' he suggests, while stressing that Adam's mother shares an equal responsibility in ultimately sparing the world from destruction. 'As parents we muddle on through and that scenario lends itself to many comic moments,' he says. 'The Youngs are very stable and Middle England. That's important in raising a good Antichrist.'

In dressing the two characters, costume designer Claire Anderson set out to embody a couple that are both dependable and consistent. She recalls her own upbringing here, when it seemed to her that all her parents' female friends dressed in a similar fashion. 'They always had the same look, like an A-line skirt and a little jumper and that sums up Mrs Young to me. She's constant and gentle.'

'Claire was very sure in what she wanted,' says Sian. 'It was a particular tone and colour, so that whenever you see Mrs Young there is a certain sense of nostalgia and connection. It's a sort of fifties wholesome era, and we don't change for eleven years! It creates a certain expectation that when you come home the world is always the same.'

Looking back on the production, both Daniel and Sian speak highly of the quality of both the script and direction.

'I was led by the amazing Douglas,' says Sian. 'He's the lynchpin. The key to it all. As actors, it means we can go with Neil's writing and trust that Douglas will push or pull us wherever we need to go.'

For Daniel Mays, his *Good Omens* experience is defined by the opportunity to work with Sian and the stellar cast present for his character's climactic appearance. 'Mr Young arrives at the airbase in his Morris Minor where all these individuals played by incredible actors are waiting there for him,' he says, referring to the moment in the story when the forces of good and evil face one another at the brink of Armageddon. 'I only had to deliver about four lines of dialogue, but I felt like I was auditioning for RADA again.'

Cars personify characters throughout *Good Omens*, from Crowley's dark, sleek Bentley to Madame Tracy's jaunty scooter... and Arthur Young's dependable Morris Minor.

ARTHUR YOUNG:
Would anyone here
care to explain to
me what exactly is
going on?

ACROSS THE CORRIDOR

In which two humans with little in common come together (for tea) and a common cause.

'**The idea was to show how two people can live in identical apartments in the same building and yet live so differently from each other.**'

UK producer Phil Collinson describes a set for the *Good Omens* shoot as if it has to be seen to be truly appreciated. On paper, two dwellings divided by a corridor shouldn't spark such enthusiasm. In reality, and in keeping with the production, the design, detail and meaning invested in the combined spaces lifts it from the mundane to the sublime.

'It was one of the best set builds I've ever stood on,' continues Phil. 'The apartments are the mirror image of each other, but contrasting in every other way. One is tidy and feminine and pink while the other is a mess. It looks like it belongs to an old guy with his mind on other things. We spend a lot of time there,' he says, 'and so we wanted to make it as visual as we could. So, you head up the stairs, turn right and it's shabby, dirty and cramped, or you turn left and it's a nice place to be.'

The first apartment Phil describes is home to a character that is memorable in the novel and unforgettable in the adaptation. In her own right, Madame Tracy is a woman of two halves. In one guise she entertains lonely gentlemen, which pretty much amounts to making cups of tea for them and listening with the occasional hug thrown in. In the other, Madame Tracy swaps her stockings and garters for the psychic's veil and endeavours to fulfil the needs of a very different kind of clientele. As a sex worker and clairvoyant, played with great relish in the TV series by Miranda Richardson, she's a kind soul who seeks to bring people comfort in an odd sort of way.

This generosity extends to her shambolic neighbour and occupant of the flat opposite. Shadwell might reject everything Madame Tracy stands for, in

For both Madame Tracy and Witchfinder Sergeant Shadwell, this grubby phone booth forms the centre of their operations.

his role as self-appointed Witchfinder Sergeant, but then this is *Good Omens*, and in *Good Omens* opposites attract. Or at least find a space in the middle where they can connect.

'It was liberating for me,' says the director of photography Gavin Finney. 'Each space was perhaps slightly bigger than it would be in real life, and so cleverly designed so we can see how they're used in completely different ways.' With the build conceived purely for filming, Gavin describes how he was able to bridge the two apartments-without-ceilings in a unique way. 'Douglas wanted us to fly over the top,' he says. 'So we start in Shadwell's flat and then follow the action over the hall into Madame Tracy's flat. The lighting for each one is very different, but these are wonderful challenges.'

For *Good Omens*' production designer Michael Ralph, the inspiration for this set build stemmed from a photography exhibition that focused purely on doors in residential tenement blocks.

'It mesmerized me,' he says. 'Each door was open, with the camera pointed through the doorway to show how that person lived inside. So every photograph offered a glimpse through the same frame into a unique world. I wanted Madame

With a corridor dividing the two flats, symbolically keeping two contrasting characters apart, Madame Tracy and Shadwell meet in the middle when Newt arrives in their lives.

Shadwell's shambolic flat reflects his character, and yet production designer Michael Ralph, foregrounds a sense of beauty in such a chaotic environment.

Across the corridor from Shadwell's, Madame Tracy's flat is the mirror image in terms of design and contrasting in every other way.

Tracy's flat and Shadwell's flat to be identical in the same way, but different worlds if you walked from one to the other.'

While the two apartments are recognizably the same on a structural level, Michael Ralph lent both his trademark twist with features that remove them one step from reality.

'I deliberately designed arches that the viewer has never seen before,' he says, 'and also fireplaces that look Georgian but they're not from that era. I invented an architecture that looks familiar but doesn't really exist!' he jokes.

Michael also manipulated each space for maximum impact on the viewer. 'I raised the corridor up five steps from each flat. So when we visit each apartment the audience has a chance to submerge into their world rather than walk in on a level.'

The task of decorating each flat to reflect the personality of the occupant also fell to Michael. In furnishing the Witchfinder Sergeant's abode, the production designer oversaw the placement of every last unwashed plate and cigarette burn as if it were an art installation.

'Shadwell lives in this shambolic nicotine-coloured, single-man dwelling. There's one chair and one lamp, and the couch is covered in so much stuff that nobody ever visits. It was phenomenally beautiful,' he says.

Turning to Madame Tracy's apartment, Michael sought to bring a range of influences together to create a whole in terms of fixtures, fittings and furnishings that was greater than the sum of its parts.

'I wanted it to be multi-religious and multi-cultural so she looks like some kind of European mystic living within a multi-coloured tapestry,' he explains. On camera it was quite incredible. Everything came together to create a tangible world.' When Madame Tracy switched from her role as mystic to sex worker, Michael reflected the transformation accordingly. 'We threw black cloths over lamps and lit candles so the light source changed,' he says.

Having created two worlds divided by a corridor, Michael Ralph joined the rest of the crew in watching these two legendary actors at work. Within their respective homes, both Miranda Richardson, who plays Madame Tracy, and Michael McKean as Shadwell come across as naturals in their roles, and it's no surprise to learn that both were first choices for Neil. Much is down to their formidable acting heritage and comic flair, but this is reinforced by the creative work of the costume, hair and make-up departments.

'Neil and Terry's writing is very succinct,' says costume designer Claire Anderson, who has previously worked on productions including *American Gods*, *Black Mirror*, *Royal Night Out* and *State of Play*. 'It means costume comes off the page very clearly for many of the characters. So in *Good Omens* we built from what we have in the story to what audience perception would be to what would look comfortable and timeless.'

In terms of dressing characters as distinct as Shadwell and Madame Tracy, Claire outlines a process that turns the script into a creative springboard. 'I meet with the producer and the director,' she says. 'I read the book, and consider factors like the fanbase because everyone has an expectation, and I also work with the actors. Then I put visual moods together for each character. Sometimes ideas get abandoned and other times it's the first idea that you roll with.'

With ideas evolved into sketches, Claire emphasizes the importance of the colour palette in defining her characters. 'Aziraphale needed to be light and cream, iridescent and ethereal,' she says, 'and Crowley had to be black.'

As for Shadwell, 'he's a grubby and dishevelled character and his colours reflect that'. Neil Gaiman had his own take, suggesting Shadwell's look should be informed by a much-loved eccentric called Stanley Green. With his placard urging 'less lust by less protein', Green was a familiar sight on London's Oxford Street from the late sixties until his death in the early nineties. In *Good Omens*, when Newt first comes across Shadwell clutching a sign with an anti-witchcraft message that could have come from a discarded draft of the Bible, Shadwell's whole stance and visual appearance might be considered as a fond homage to the 'Protein Man'. Shadwell's jacket, however, is what truly defines his look.

'As he came from the witchfinder route I wanted elements of uniform about him,' explains Claire, who subsequently trawled through history in assembling a suitable look. 'I created a moodboard full of witchfinders and used that to influence the shape and style of his clothing. We went for a Barbour jacket

DONATION OF WITCHFINDER

Col. Mackinnion
as used in Uig
during the witch alarms of 1899

The Witchfinder at work. Shadwell's tools of the trade, from the maps that take him to Tadfield, along with the lapel badges of office to an original witch bell.

with a cape and a fishing bag which has a slightly timeless oddness about it. We then adorned it all as Neil and Terry had written, with badges made from everything from assorted wine labels to tin labels on chains that hang off whisky bottles.' Claire describes the range of details in her costume work with great enthusiasm. 'It helps the audience determine what family each character belongs to,' she says. 'It's semiotics.'

In dressing Madame Tracy, Claire Anderson took the view that she was dealing with two characters.

'You can tell what people do from what they're wearing. She's a part-time mystic and a sex worker. So it was easy! I gave her a flowing gown and colours that make her look kooky,' says Claire, describing Madame Tracy's psychic guise before explaining how she dressed her in a flamboyant kimono for her scenes as a lady of the night. 'Then, for the scooter ride to Tadfield I harked back to the traditional helmet and a cape which is in fact a Welsh tapestry blanket. I have a magpie eye,' she adds, 'and this is a production where I can be wide-ranging and free. Nobody belongs in real time. Even Madame Tracy has something of the 1960s about her, which is something Neil wanted to see. Most of the stuff

As the series costume designer it was important that Claire Anderson, seen here looking on as Miranda and Michael prepare to shoot a scene over a pot of tea, was on hand throughout filming.

is made specially,' Claire adds. 'You can't just nip to the shops and buy it, which is why fantasy costume is so enjoyable. It's better than Jane Austen as it's new and fresh and exciting to explore.'

Nosh Oldham has an equally big influence on each character's appearance. As the *Good Omens* hair and make-up designer, her CV boasts productions including *Downton Abbey*, *Luther* and *Strike*, based on the detective novels by Robert Galbraith aka J. K. Rowling.

'I do a lot of period stuff, but I started in blood and guts,' says Nosh breezily, referring to her early work on films such as Antonia Bird's 1999 black comedy horror, *Ravenous*.

Working closely with costume designer Claire Anderson, 'so the head fits the body', as she sees it, Nosh Oldham seized upon the opportunity provided by Douglas Mackinnon, who invited her to be bold.

'It was a huge canvas,' she says, 'and I aimed to be striking, quirky and unusual. Working with a period drama can be restricting to a point, but *Good Omens* goes from Adam and Eve onwards. It meant I could pretty much take my inspiration from anywhere – every place and time.'

Beginning with mood boards, Nosh works by collaborating with the main cast and evolving a singular look for each one. In particular, she says, working with Miranda Richardson was a joyful experience.

'She's spectacular in every possible way,' she says. 'Very creative and visual as well. So for the psychic Madame Tracy we looked at portraits of women by the German painter, Otto Dix. Together, we thought that she would work rather well with wrapped-up hair, red and finger-waved, and extravagant make-up. Then, when Miranda was playing the naughty girl, who we called "Sexy Time", we went for the seaside picture-postcard look. It was quite doll-like with the sixties vibe, and we stuck closely to that.' Nosh stresses how each look had to be distinctive. 'Madame Tracy plays these roles as part of her job,' she says. 'She's a character playing characters, and Miranda had a lot of input. She was great fun, and we agreed on a look that gelled with what we had in mind.'

For each character, Nosh creates a hair and make-up mood board from a wide and diverse range of media to provide a visual starting point for the look.

Aziraphale's board is predominately white and silver in theme, with images of a silver-haired David Lynch and diaphanous platinum blondes, while black imagery dominates Crowley's board along with close-ups of reptilian eyes.

'It's a mangle of stuff, but depends on who you're given,' Nosh explains. 'Shadwell was a divine creature, who I made look like the nicotine man. In the script he smokes a lot and takes too much sugar, and so I felt he should look unwell. I also "nicotined" his fingers and face so that you could see he was a real smoker. Michael was great with it all,' she adds. 'He grew his hair, which we left unwashed, and went unshaved. The more an actor can give us like that, the easier it is.'

With the set dressed and the characters complete, it was Miranda Richardson who provided what many crew members consider to be the most entertaining shoot in the vast schedule.

'It was the scene of one of the most memorable moments,' Nosh says, referring to the séance Madame Tracy hosts in Episode Five for clients including Mrs Ormerod, Mr Scroggie and Julia Petley. Once the colourful medium has reminded them that her spirit guide needs twenty-five pounds, it should be a routine commune with the afterlife, and in particular Mrs Ormerod's husband, as she wants to tell him about some broken guttering. However, it takes an unexpected turn when the discorporated Aziraphale makes a spirited appearance as an angel in need of a body to inhabit so that he can reach Tadfield and head off Armageddon. Having already materialized live on air in the body of an American television evangelist, somewhat uselessly in Florida, the angel comes to occupy the medium and sex worker with riotous results.

'It was a lovely period of work,' says first assistant director Cesco Reidy. 'Miranda was a delight, and Michael is absolutely brilliant. With Miranda in charge of the crystal ball, the séance made us laugh on the floor more than anything else. Just to be on the set that day will stay with me for a long time. It was high comedy. Just very, very funny.'

'In true *Good Omens* style, that scene was totally off the wall,' agrees script supervisor Jemima Thomas. 'Miranda went for it with the most amazing performance. Douglas asked for a ten and she gave it eleven.'

Out of hours. Madame Tracy's flat was designed to change in terms of lighting and soft furnishing to reflect the nature of her role either as a sex worker or psychic medium. A bed piled high with pink and fluffy toys signals she's off duty while her reference books and crystal ball create an air of clairvoyant chintz.

MADAME TRACY

MIRANDA RICHARDSON

'She's a vessel!'

 On summing up her *Good Omens* character so succinctly, Miranda Richardson hoots with laughter. It's a fair assessment of Madame Tracy's dual profession as a psychic and sex worker, but when Miranda sees the funny side of something she doesn't hold back. In many ways, it's also a reflection of her approach to a character that she considers with great fondness.

'In both her jobs, Madame Tracy provides a service,' she says to expand. 'She offers assistance to people, but she's not a charlatan. It's not her intention to fleece anyone. She's a proper performer, investing in what she's doing at the time without confusing one job over the other. But in each role she's helpful, and that comes from a good place.'

Miranda Richardson rose to fame in the 1985 film *Dance with a Stranger*, and earned critical acclaim with performances in *The Crying Game*, *Damage* and *Stronger* among many others. Placed at the top of the wish list to play Madame Tracy by director Douglas Mackinnon, Miranda joined the production without previously reading the novel or being aware of its fan base.

'It turns out I am illiterate,' she says with more laughter. 'I was familiar with Neil's work somewhat, but I hadn't read any Terry Pratchett, and this is remiss of me. I need to catch up.'

On reading the scripts, however, Miranda knew she wanted to be involved in the production. 'It's funny. It's fresh. That's it, really,' she says simply. 'You just get a feeling, a buzz, and think, "This one is a keeper." And the idea of Madame Tracy's double life was rather irresistible,' she adds.

Having joined the *Good Omens* family, how did she find her way into the role?

'For me, costume and make-up is a big part of it. I know that's external, but it's also important. It's how Madame Tracy dresses for an occasion, and she does have a sense of occasion. It helps her and it's what her clientele expects. Even though it's based very much in reality there is a heightened aspect to it,' she points out. 'So we were able to have fun with colour. And her abode is lovely. When I saw the pictures of the set I was going to be working on I felt it couldn't be better. Shadwell's flat is equally amazing,' she adds, referring to the run-down space across the corridor that contrasts with Madame Tracy's abode but creates a fittingly neutral zone for them to meet in the middle. 'Part of my personality is Shadwell,' says Miranda. 'I can see myself inhabiting that space as well.' Like Aziraphale and Crowley, superficially the two characters are polar opposites, and yet they share a deep connection underneath based upon a love of humanity.

In Episode Five, it's Aziraphale who quite literally inhabits Madame Tracy's body. Having accidentally spirited himself to Heaven, the angel possesses the psychic and sex worker during a séance in a desperate bid to track down the Antichrist before he fulfils his destiny. Terry Pratchett and Neil Gaiman achieve this to great effect in the novel, with Aziraphale's spirit taking shape inside Madame Tracy before they race off on a scooter possessed, but how does it translate to the screen?

'It was like having a good workout on some occasions,' Miranda jokes, referring to the physically demanding sequence in which her character absorbs the spirit of the angel. The resulting manifestation of two roles in one, she says, was a collaborative effort. 'As a platform for me, I enlisted Michael Sheen's help to record in advance how he might say certain things,' she explains. 'We went through the scenes together, and did a couple of permutations of how he might say a line or act in particular situations, which I found very helpful. It was about assuming his mannerisms in a way, and his tone of voice, but it's only in flashes as most of the time she's being herself. Aziraphale just comes through on occasions.' Miranda feels the effect was further heightened by the fact that the angel's character is so different to that of Madame Tracy. 'She's dressed as she would dress but there is another persona within her. So you've got this particularity of her look, with massive false eyelashes, and Aziraphale's rather genteel manner.'

'Madame Tracy has two very different looks.
You can't mix them up,' says Nosh Oldham,
on the sex worker (top) and psychic medium
(bottom). In addition, Nosh worked with
Claire Anderson on yet another look for
when she zips off on her scooter.

MADAME TRACY:
I don't do
anything kinky
except by prior
agreement, and
my knees aren't
what they were.

MADAME TRACY: You'll need an extra five pounds for a sandwich and a coffee...

When telling me about Madame Tracy's relationship with Shadwell, who considers his neighbour to be the devil incarnate, Miranda Richardson is clear what's really behind his animosity.

'They've known each other a long time, and she's grown to care about him over a couple of years. As far as Shadwell's concerned she's always there, and probably represents the thing that frightens him most.' If the friendship has always existed under the surface, Miranda speaks warmly of the way in which it rises up through *Good Omens*. 'He befriends her and protects her and nobody has done that for a while. She's probably seen everything in her two professions. She knows you don't judge a book by its cover, and that people have hidden depths. I think she's probably rather a good psychologist,' she suggests.

In Neil Gaiman's view, mindful of the fact that she is one of the few humans in a narrative populated by angels and demons, Madame Tracy represents 'the heart of the story'. Miranda agrees, finding the role an honour.

'It's quite a thing to carry, but I like her very much. She's a good egg. She brings people comfort spiritually and sexually.' As for working with Neil, Miranda speaks

ABOVE: Shadwell refuses Madame Tracy's offer to pay his train fare to Tadfield from her ill-gotten gains. OPPOSITE: In Neil's own words, Madame Tracy represents 'the heart of *Good Omens*, in an odd sort of way, both her professions are about bringing people comfort'.

As Armageddon approaches, Madame Tracy finds herself hosting the spirit of Aziraphale. In preparing for this dual role, Miranda Richardson consulted Michael Sheen on how the angel might deliver particular lines. As for handling Shadwell's Thundergun, this is a weapon with a life of its own.

MADAME TRACY: Sometimes I think it might be nice to move out of London. Get a little bungalow. And they say that two can live as cheaply as one... and it would be nice to have a man around...

highly not just of the quality of his scripts but his role as showrunner. 'Neil is a wonderful praiser, and a trustworthy praiser,' she says. 'He also asked me to perform my version of Madame Tracy, and that was very liberating.'

From her stand-out scene hosting the séance to piloting a flying scooter with the spirit of an angel inhabiting her, Miranda Richardson delivers a full-throttle performance to a character previously only pictured in the mind of the reader. Does she feel any sense of expectation from those familiar with the novel? Having appeared in another book adaptation, *Harry Potter and the Goblet of Fire*, Miranda has faith in the process of transforming a story from page to screen.

'I did what I could in that,' she says of her role as journalist Rita Skeeter, 'and a lot of people were saying that's exactly how they saw her. So I think there's a willingness to go along with it,' she adds, referring to *Good Omens*. 'A lot of care has been taken on how it's presented, and the production values are great. It's an extravaganza and should be as much fun to watch as it has been to make.

Sometimes it takes an unearthly crisis to bring a couple together.

SHADWELL

MICHAEL McKEAN

'Lurk!'

Michael McKean has just offered up a word to me that he claims to struggle with when speaking in his character's Scottish accent. To the untrained ear, it sounds as perfect as Michael's English accent playing the vocalist and guitarist David St Hubbins in the classic 1984 spoof rock mockumentary, *Spinal Tap*. The award-winning American actor is as versatile with voices as he is with the range of characters he's played across four decades, from roles in *Best in Show* to *Better Call Saul*, and as a regular on *Saturday Night Live*.

In playing the Witchfinder Sergeant who finds himself on the frontline to save the world as Armageddon approaches, Michael McKean has embraced a character that showcases his talents to the full. 'We fall in love with Shadwell slowly,' Neil Gaiman has written about the character. 'He's misguided, but he cares.' Michael identifies with this view, and explains how he came to understand Shadwell's hidden charms.

'Sometimes I go into a part feeling one way about it, and discover other things along the way,' he begins. 'Half way through the process I came to realize that Witchfinder Sergeant Shadwell has been clinging to his own survival via virtue of his imaginary righteousness. He thinks that he's saving the world, but seen objectively he could be viewed as a conman, as a guy who just has these couple of people who keep him going, and not on very much. One runs a bookshop. The other is a gentleman who he meets sometimes in out-of-the-way places who he assumes is connected with the mob. All he wants out of it is a few bucks to keep his imaginary squad of witchfinders going. Really it's just going into his pocket, but he's not getting rich from it. He's just scraping by, and honestly believes that he's on the side of the angels. And he is, it turns out, but no one is more surprised than Shadwell when he discovers that evil really is afoot in the world, and that Armageddon is something that one can fight against, rather than just make blue-sky comments about.'

In talking about his *Good Omens* character, it's clear that Michael McKean has grappled with every aspect of Shadwell's existence in order to truly connect with him.

'He's just got out of stir when we see him as a young man,' he says, referring to our first encounter with his younger incarnation in the back room of a Soho pub in Episode Three. 'We don't look closely at what landed him in there, but he's found a way to survive on the edges of reality, and people are willing to keep him afloat with witchfinding. Shadwell comes to believe in what he's doing, and part of that is down to the fact that he doesn't have a lot else in his life. What started as a small-time scam for an ex-con has become a small-time career. One that is good enough for a lonely guy. As for his relationship with Madame Tracy, she's the lady across the hall whose means of self-support are questionable. On the one hand, he believes she's a sex worker though doesn't want to know, and on the other she claims to be a medium. If so then she's working with dark forces, and that's something Shadwell won't tolerate. But he does so as she does a lot for him in terms of messages, cooking meals and shoring up the rent if the money isn't there.'

Michael also considers the flourishing of their unusual relationship to be one more seam in *Good Omens*' moral bedrock. 'We don't always recognize the angels in our lives, because we might mistake them for something else,' he says, 'but they're there. I've met a few in my life. In fact, I'm married to one.' Michael further illustrates his point by referring to his involvement in a theatre project that aims to rehabilitate prisoners through the arts. 'I went along to meet their cast, and I met some angels. The women who run it are remarkable,' he continues. 'They believe in the notion that redemption is possible, and it's one of those things I can't live without. It wasn't until we were working on *Good Omens* – in particular Madame Tracy's relationship with Shadwell – that I realized it's exactly what's going on here. Redemption is our favourite story,' he finishes. 'From *High Noon* to *Star Wars*.'

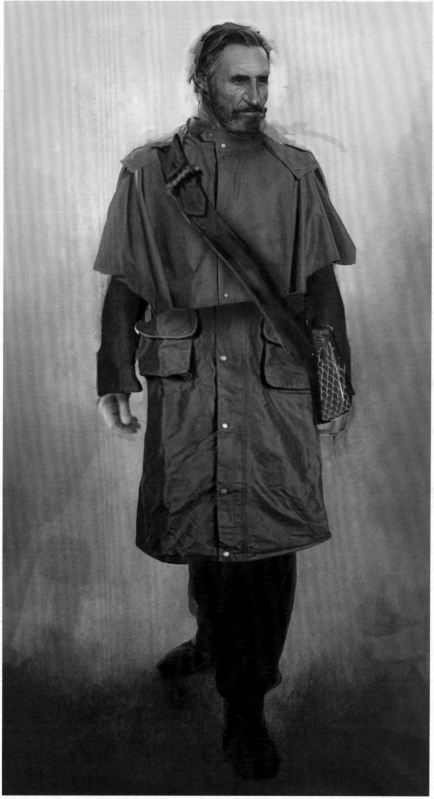

Some character costumes were designed ahead of casting, as illustrated here by Claire Anderson's sketch for Witchfinder Sergeant Shadwell. While the Barbour stockman coat was established at this stage, Michael McKean brought his own brand of dishevelment and charm to the role.

SHADWELL:
Don't thank me.
I'm the thin red
line that stands
between humanity
and the darkness,
but don't thank me.

Madame Tracy might see hidden virtues in her neighbour, but is her fellow human in the *Good Omens* story on the side of good or evil? Despite considering himself to be standing 'between humanity and the darkness', Shadwell's not averse to accepting commissions from Crowley in his role as Witchfinder Sergeant. Whether Shadwell's aware that he's in the pay of a demon is teasingly left to our imagination, but Michael believes we should just enjoy the ride.

'Shadwell falls through realities very quickly,' observes Michael. 'So he barely has time to make a judgement call. He's thrown in his lot with a sex worker and medium next door who he's been referring to as a Whore of Babylon, and found himself drawn into this strange battle, but he doesn't pick sides. He just knows there's something going on, and doesn't realize that he's falling in love with Madame Tracy. He's just the man who finds himself with the thundergun in his hand and the sky opening up in front of him, and does what he can.'

Shadwell also does what he can for a young man seeking direction early on in the story. What does his adoption of Newt Pulsifer tell us about his character?

'He sees a kindred spirit,' says Michael. 'There's something in Newt that he identifies with that tells him they're fighting the same fight. It's a completely

ABOVE: Neil loosely based Shadwell's first appearance in *Good Omens* on Stanley Green, a well-known human billboard in London's West End through the eighties and nineties who extolled the virtues of 'protein wisdom'. OPPOSITE: The Sergeant in his headquarters.

SHADWELL: Off ye go, Witchfinder Private Pulsifer. May the armies of glory march beside ye.

fraudulent picture of how he was as a younger man, because Shadwell has forgotten the hustle angle. Now, he's a righteous warrior who is actually scraping by, and would starve to death without Madame Tracy, and taking on Newt as his apprentice gives him a sense of responsibility. Shadwell assumes that without his help Newt will fall into the hands of witches such as Anathema, and somehow he'll lose his soul. Newt would probably be fine without his help, and frankly few would want to gather under Shadwell's wing. It's dingy under there!'

The sense of misguided self-belief that burns inside the character is endearing and amusing in equal measure. Michael identifies with the small man caught up in a grand scheme. He attributes much of this to a grounding in sci-fi and a late shine for the work of Terry Pratchett.

'I've read a bunch of *Discworld* novels and I'm glad I have a bunch to go,' he says, 'I love the idea of building a universe, not taking it very seriously and seeing the comic possibilities in the grand ideas. It's really refreshing. There are deep ideas floating around in there.'

Given he seems to have found his natural role in Shadwell, it comes as a surprise to learn that Michael was originally slated to play a different character.

'I had become friendly with Neil via Twitter, and traded bits of information about our lives,' he begins. 'My wife and I are the corniest couple in the world, for example. We read to each other at night, and two of our favourites are *The Graveyard Book* and *The Ocean at the End of the Lane*. When I messaged Neil about this, he answered that he reads extracts from his work in progress to his wife (the American musician and performance artist Amanda Palmer) as she's falling asleep, and the next day she tells him her last thoughts before drifting off. It's like Thomas Edison, who used to take naps holding ball bearings over a metal pan. As he fell asleep the ball bearings would drop into the pan and wake him up so he could record his thoughts. He felt that there is an area of creativity between dreams and waking, as does Neil, who described this to me in his response. Then, having connected in this way, he offered me a cameo in the series as a televangelist folk singer.'

Michael willingly accepted, only for the situation to change when the author himself came to watch him in a play on Broadway. 'Around the time of the

... and then heads off after his new employee because Newt might need help in defeating the dark forces at work there.

SHADWELL: What would you say... if I told you that this hand had just Exorcised a Demon, clean off the surface of the Earth...?

Shadwell informs Madame Tracy that he appears to possess supernatural powers.

intermission,' he says, 'Neil came and told me that he had another role in mind for me, and asked if I could do a Scottish accent.'

Of course, anyone familiar with the novel will know that Shadwell's roots are famously hard to pin down. Neil Gaiman explains why the decision was taken to root him north of the border.

'In the book, Shadwell has a strange accent that careers around the country. It's unplaceable. It also doesn't get nicer in any of them,' he adds, 'but while it works on the page we decided it sounded distracting on screen, like an actor who can't nail a voice. So we made him a Scot who's been living in the south for the best part of fifty years.' At the same time, both Neil and Michael McKean jokily acknowledge that final judgement on the quality of Shadwell's accent in the adaption must fall to native Scot Douglas Mackinnon who was born and raised on the Isle of Skye.

'How did I cope?' Douglas refects. 'If anyone wants to come at me and say that's not a Scottish accent, they would be right. I wouldn't call it a Scottish accent, that's for sure.'

'It's a glorious accent,' offers Neil in mock defence. 'Whatever it is.'

'Douglas chided me if I didn't get it right,' laughs Michael, who adds that he thrived on the director's sardonic humour. 'He'd throw Scottishisms at me that made no sense, just to see my face fall.'

Talking to Michael McKean about his *Good Omens* experience, and his rapport with the likes of Douglas and Neil, it's evident he's enjoyed every moment. He recounts each high point of his time with a sparkle in both his voice and his eyes, and it's clear to me that he's relished the experience. Michael is a natural raconteur, and lyrical when it comes to describing his character's unique journey through the *Good Omens* story.

'I'm working with Miranda Richardson,' he says, as if that's all he needs to add. Michael remembers the moment he tried on Shadwell's oilskin greatcoat, created by Claire Anderson. He knew this was a part that worked for him. It was 'like gold' he says now. 'Shadwell is a guy who is his own army. With his badges and armbands he has designed himself from the outside. Everything Claire gave me worked, which helped me to find the character, as did the quality of the script. I could see how he would react to the finger,' he adds, referring to the turning point for his character on witnessing Aziraphale conversing with God's phantasmagorical floating-head spokesperson, the Metatron. Believing he is witnessing witchcraft in the first degree, Shadwell points at Aziraphale accusingly, only for the angel to step back and vanish in a ring of light. While Aziraphale has in fact accidentally ascended to Heaven, the moment leaves Shadwell believing that he has acquired divine powers that can be delivered through one righteously pointed digit. 'This is his prize for a life of self-delusion,' adds Michael, 'and he's not sure he can handle it. It's like having the adrenalin rush that you're worried might turn into a heart attack.'

Michael McKean is as amusing as he is entertaining, and an actor with an ability to combine comedy and tragedy into one character. Watching him perform as Shadwell the Witchfinder Sergeant, alongside Jack Whitehall's Newton Pulsifer and Miranda Richardson's Madame Tracy, we see what it means to be human in a grand power play between good and evil, and root for a man despite his flaws.

A BRIEF HISTORY OF INHUMANITY

In which Aziraphale and Crowley witness man's capacity to do evil unto his own kind.

Where most television drama productions might devote the first minute or so to a moment or a scene before the opening credits roll, *Good Omens* takes things not just one step further but way beyond all expectation.

In Episode Three, what Douglas Mackinnon and Neil Gaiman fondly refer to as the 'pre-title sequence' lasts for half the show. It's a departure from the novel, and one of the most ambitious, inventive and stylistically wide-ranging series of events in the *Good Omens* adaptation. Here, we follow the immortal demon and the angel through turbulent events in history as they seek to sway things in the name of good or evil and conclude that one cancels out the other. We begin as the animals file two by two – and in size order – into the Ark, then jump to Golgotha and the Crucifixion of Christ. From there, Aziraphale and Crowley crop up in Ancient Rome, Arthurian England and then at a production of *Hamlet* with Shakespeare himself, before romping through Revolutionary France, Victorian England and on towards a church during the Blitz as a bomb drops out of the sky before finally settling in sixties Soho. The result is dizzying in scope and genre, and threaded together seamlessly by the presence of our two lead characters as they figure out their place in the world.

The origins of the sequence, according to Neil Gaiman, stem from an obstacle he encountered as he wrote that is common to screenwriters when they are adapting from a novel. For what might work wonders on the page doesn't always translate to screen.

'When I broke down the plot into six episodes,' he says, 'one thing that became apparent was that Crowley and Aziraphale had nothing to do in

Douglas shot the Crucifixion scene towards sundown so the low light lengthened shadows and created striking silhouettes.

Episode Three. It has to do with the strange way in which the book is written, in which we bring on other characters instead such as the Them and switch to the scene at a nuclear power station,' he says, referring to the discovery that the reactor has vanished; one of a string of strange events including the emergence of Atlantis from the waves, as Adam's fanciful but all-powerful thoughts as the Antichrist child in waiting become reality. 'Meanwhile, Aziraphale sits in his bookshop and reads *The Nice and Accurate Prophecies of Agnes Nutter*,' Neil continues. 'So, I thought to myself, OK, because I love them and they're our stars, then I'll give them something to do. Let's follow them through the ages,' he says of what would be the starting point for the sequence.

In translating the novel for the screen in this way, by spinning off from the original narrative, Neil says he was deeply mindful of his late co-writer but also willing to trust his creative instinct and experience.

'It takes confidence to keep the kinetic energy while doing a flashback,' he suggests. 'I needed almost thirty years off from *Good Omens* before I attempted it, and I also needed the ghost of Terry to say, "Here, I am giving you this torch. Don't drop it." If it hadn't been for Terry actually asking me to adapt the novel

A Biblical bromance. The 'pre-title sequence' in Episode Three of *Good Omens* effectively charts the friendship between a demon and an angel from Old Testament times to the modern age.

then I wouldn't have done it,' Neil adds. 'So, I thought if I'm going to make the ghost of Terry Pratchett proud, even though he didn't believe in ghosts, then he had to trust me to do it.'

According to Douglas Mackinnon, every scene from history that follows in the pre-title sequence is threaded through by an exploration of our capacity to kill each other and the gods we worship.

'There is also a bigger strand,' the director says of the same sequence, 'which examines Aziraphale's relationship with Crowley and how it has developed over six thousand years. So they keep on ending up in the same place at the same time where one is doing something good while the other is doing something bad, which cancels each other out. They realize if they do nothing then it'll even out in the end and Heaven and Hell won't notice, but clearly it's about their relationship, and some would say their love affair. I know Michael Sheen is a hundred per cent sure that Aziraphale falls in love with Crowley,' Douglas offers, 'and that moment occurs when the bomb drops on the church.'

With Michael Ralph's detailed production design in evidence throughout, the pre-title sequence is rich in meaning and entirely open to interpretation. Stylistically, how did Douglas approach this chain of scenes in which each one is so far apart from the next in history?

'I trust that I know what *Good Omens* looks like,' he says. 'One of the key points in directing, and helping the audience, is that each time we arrive in a new place we set it up as if telling a joke. So, with Noah, I start with a wide shot of the Ark and the animals going in so people know where it is before our guys show up and have a conversation. With every new place, I've tried to hold the audience's hand. I don't want to mystify them; I want them to feel confident about where they are.'

Each link in the sequence is directed with a nod to a particular genre, from a Crucifixion scene that echoes Cecil B. DeMille's 1956 biblical epic, *The Ten Commandments*, to the stark light and shadow reminiscent of forties noir classic, *The Maltese Falcon*, when we arrive at the wartime spy encounter in a church aisle. In doing so, Douglas was keenly aware of the line between homage and pastiche, having worked on the frontline directing *Doctor Who*.

The Crucifixion scene doesn't shy away from the visceral nature of Christ's death. At the same time, Douglas set out to capture the moment with sensitivity and respect.

'A lot of that is genre-based,' he says. 'As a director, there is a ledge you need to drive towards, but if you go too far you're into pastiche, and so you take it as close to the line as you can. It has to be truthful and honest, which means in *Good Omens* I want people to believe we are dealing with angels, but there is a point where you can trip and go into high comedy.'

Douglas tells a story in which a Briton and an American visit Disneyland. 'The American goes, "Look! It's Mickey!" while the Brit says, "Look at that idiot in the mouse suit!" Well, somewhere in the middle is *Good Omens*. When we present an angel then it's an angel. There is no sideways look.' His approach to directing the show is to play it straight, and with great conviction, and let any satirical or comic moments breathe from the characters within that setting.

This seriousness of purpose is immediately apparent in every scene that forms the pre-title sequence. Having worked alongside Douglas in the director's tent for every shoot in the sequence, script supervisor Jemima Thomas explains how his commitment to treating every scene with gravity and respect created a sense of cohesion.

'What I love is that all these different moments are little vignettes,' she begins. 'They are stories in their own right, and we did it all on a grand scale rather than playing it for comedy. In the Crucifixion scene, for example, we shot a close-up of the nail going through Christ's hand. It's an awful moment, but countered by Crowley wincing. Everything is shot seriously, but the script is funny, and that's what makes it sharper.'

The Crucifixion scene was filmed on a windswept plain just outside Cape Town at sunset. Watching Roman soldiers haul Christ's crucifix into position, with a hundred extras and a blood-red sun setting in the background, proved to be both a moving and unsettling experience for cast and crew.

'It looked like how it might have been carried out,' says first assistant director Cesco Reidy. 'We had the two thieves laid out on crosses on either side of Christ, and using special effects hammered nails through his feet and hands. Raising the cross is a two-step process, where the soldiers get them to hand height and then use poles to lift them upright into position. It's then you realize that crucifixion really does what it's designed to do,' he points out.

'Even when you're pretending, with tiny supports under the actors' heels, it puts a tremendous stress on the body.'

In discussing the meaning within this particular scene, Douglas explains that his outlook on religion provided him with a revealing lens.

'I'm an atheist,' he says, 'but I wanted to treat it with the utmost respect. So Jesus is on the cross and he's suffering incredibly, but whoever he was his message is to be kind to each other. What an amazing message – which as an atheist is hamstrung by the fact that people call it supernatural. But it doesn't make the message bad. It's wonderful.'

The Crucifixion was just the beginning of a wide-ranging week in South Africa in which the production covered much of the pre-title sequence. 'We also shot Noah's Ark as well as the scenes in Ancient Rome, Revolutionary France and the Second World War in the church,' recalls Cesco. 'In effect we hopped around through thousands of years within a six-day shoot and got it all done.'

In keeping with Douglas Mackinnon's bid to capture as much footage 'in camera' for the sake of authenticity, the crew shot the Ark scene using as many live-action elements as possible.

'We had animals from camels down to sheep brought in by handlers,' says Cesco, 'We then filmed another shot further along the line where the camera is down by the feet of Aziraphale and Crowley. This time, we're looking at even smaller animals, like mice and moles, as they make their way two-by-two towards the Ark. These were real,' he stresses, although anything bigger at the front of the queue was digitally added by Milk VFX in post-production. 'Which was a wise move,' he adds.

For the director of photography, Gavin Finney, the pre-title sequence presented a visual challenge.

'It's full of transitions, and each one needed to look different,' he says. 'They're films within films, but given the right people and resources it's exciting.' Talking to Gavin about the sequence, it's clear that he thrived on meeting and exceeding the director's commitment to getting the very best possible shots throughout.

'Douglas will not settle for less than great. His bar is really high and he's maintained that. He'll talk things over until everyone is on board. As a result,' he says of the kinetic creativity at play, 'we didn't have one day where there

Aziraphale and Crowley bump into one another at a bar whilst pursuing separate missions in Ancient Rome – taming Nero and tempting Caligula.

When the demon and the angel meet in Arthurian Britain, Douglas wreathed the scene in mist so thick that the two sides barely see each other until they come face to face.

is a static camera pointing at an actor at a table, which is why everyone was buzzing. It was such fun to shoot, and it has to be said that David Tennant and Michael Sheen are brilliant together. They're so gorgeous to watch. And we don't set things up for a pratfall. The sequence is just about them living through life and weird stuff happens. It's very serious for everyone. They're trying to save the world, after all.'

'It's also an example of what films can't do,' Gavin continues. 'At ninety minutes, there's just not enough time to show a relationship over six thousand years. What's great about the TV format, which has come of age in a way, is that you can explore a novel and a novel's-worth of relationships. Finally, top actors and directors are attracted to the medium now because they've got the budget to realize that level of ambition.'

In considering a favourite moment from the pre-title sequence, Gavin Finney smiles broadly. 'Arthurian England,' he says, referring to one of the scenes shot in the UK. Gavin's pick opens with knights in armour on horseback staging a face off. 'It was so thick with smoke that Aziraphale and Crowley can hardly see each other. We made it part *Excalibur* and part *Monty Python*.'

In shooting such a large-scale scene, first assistant director Cesco Reidy notes that one element proved to be a happy accident. 'While we had to cover a large area with fog, which was a practical challenge to get the consistency of the look, we found that a water tower in the background looked like a turret from some huge unseen castle if we lined up the camera in a particular way. There was no need to add anything to it,' says Cesco. 'It looked the part.'

Throughout the shoot, *Good Omens*' script editor Charlotte Webber was on hand to advise and assist Neil in incorporating changes and refinements to the scripts. She explains how both Neil and Douglas were committed to making sure no corners were cut in the filming of the pre-title sequence, and found creative ways to stay within the budget.

'A lot of those scenes came in and went back,' she explains. 'In the end we had them all. The execution during Revolutionary France is a great example.' Citing the sheer scale of the proposed guillotine scene, and the potential cost involved, Charlotte says the pair worked together to find a solution that worked

Having made the mistake of visiting France dressed as an aristocrat, Aziraphale prepares to meet his maker once more in Episode Three's French Revolution scene. Fortunately for him, Crowley is on hand to save the day. With the angel free from his chains, Aziraphale wisely changes his outfit to blend with the revolutionaries.

for everyone. 'It was a combination of Neil insisting that it couldn't be cut, Douglas suggesting an interior version, and Neil coming up with the solution, which was to set the scene in a dungeon with the execution audible through the window.'

In a further bid for efficiency, and thanks to the transformative work of the production designer Michael Ralph, Douglas and the *Good Omens* crew were able to shoot the Bastille vignette on the set that had been used twenty-four hours earlier for the scene in Ancient Rome.

'The conversion was down to economy and necessity,' explains Cesco Reidy. 'Neil took a photo on his phone as we were setting up the Rome scene, which captured the smoky atmosphere from the incense sticks, and it looks like a beautiful painting.'

Another highlight of the sequence for many of the cast and crew was filmed at Shakespeare's Globe, the reconstruction of an Elizabethan playhouse on London's Southbank. According to Cesco, it was a chance to recreate a moment in history featuring the Bard himself, played by the waspishly comic Reece Shearsmith, while using cutting-edge filming techniques.

In pursuit of authenticity at every opportunity, the *Good Omens* production was able to shoot the *Hamlet* scene at Shakespeare's Globe – the London home of the Bard himself.

'It evolved into a fantastically funny scene,' he says, 'in which Shakespeare is present, and Aziraphale and Crowley are watching a rendition of *Hamlet*. The trouble is nobody has come to see it bar a couple of people. It isn't going down well at all, and Shakespeare is bemoaning the situation.'

Cesco explains that filming at such a historically important location is carefully controlled. With time restrictions in place, Cesco, Douglas and select crew members arrived ahead of the main shoot. 'We got the drone up,' says Cesco. 'By looking at the monitor, we were able to view what the drone was seeing and then drop it in to focus on the stage. In a way, we started filming before filming began. It's a sensitive location, but we treated the building with respect throughout the work that followed, and I'm told everyone was happy. *Good Omens* is a tidy production,' he points out. 'We like to be invited back to places.'

Fans of *The League of Gentlemen* will be pleased to discover that Reece Shearsmith isn't the only member of the darkly comic ensemble to put in a *Good Omens* cameo. Steve Pemberton and Mark Gatiss also make an appearance in the pre-title sequence, which is the first time since a special episode of

Behind the scenes with Shakespeare. Reece puts in a fine performance as the playwright frustrated by his lack of recognition.

The League of Gentlemen's pre-title sequence takeover continues inside a church during the Blitz. Here, Mark Gattis and Steve Pemberton play Nazi spies Mr Harmony and Mr Glozier, who along with Greta Kleischmidt (Niamh Walsh) double-cross a demon and an angel and pay the ultimate price.

In a pub backroom during London's swinging sixties, Crowley and associates meet a young Shadwell for the first time.

Horrible Histories that the trio have appeared together outside of Royston Vasey. Performing as Nazi spies who have arranged to meet a certain rare-book dealer in a London church during the Blitz, the pair steal the scene with the same panache as Reece's Shakespeare.

'Steve and I basically play Sydney Greenstreet and Peter Lorre,' says Mark Gatiss with a nod to two of the stars of the 1941 film noir *The Maltese Falcon*, the style of which the scene emulates. 'That's essentially how it's written and pitched, and as it's set in London during the Second World War, naturally we filmed it in Cape Town,' he says playfully referencing a decision based on production logistics and the fact that the city offered a church with a suitably looming interior.

In the scene, under the Nazis' aerial assault on the English capital, Mark Gatiss's Harmony and Steve Pemberton's Glozier are hoping to acquire Agnes Nutter's book of prophecies for the Führer himself. What follows, in a tense exchange with one Mr A. Z. Fell, does not go to plan for the spies, or indeed Aziraphale, when the whistle of a falling bomb seizes their attention. From start to explosive finish, the scene is portrayed with absolute sincerity and devotion to the noir genre. There's no hint that anyone is playing it with tongue in cheek, which makes this little black and white homage all the more endearing.

'I am too tall to be Peter Lorre but I did it with the voice and slid the vowels around,' says Mark on his approach to the scene. 'The odd thing about Lorre is that for all his Hollywoodishness he's Austro-Hungarian which makes his accent unplaceable.' Mark chuckles to himself. 'Well, that's my excuse, but it was a joy to do.'

The fact that Agnes Nutter's prophecies are rooted in the esoteric and arcane is something that naturally appeals to Mark. He talks with great interest about the Nazis' obsession with the occult, their alleged pursuit of artefacts such as the Spear of Destiny and the Grail, and references *Indiana Jones and the Last Crusade*. When it comes to the subject of the Dark Arts and its representation in popular media, Mark Gatiss is a font of knowledge. 'Our scene is a Dennis Wheatley section really,' he says with a nod to the late occult-thriller writer whose bestselling novels included *The Devil Rides Out*.

As well as being a stand-out moment stylistically, the scene was written especially by Neil Gaiman for the TV series.

'It's liberating,' says Mark about the fact that the scene has no roots in the novel. 'It means you don't hang on expectations, and the fact is Neil has been free with the text which is what you need to do with an adaptation anyway. It's an old-fashioned problem for fans, but I think it's good to go in without a hangover about what they're *not* doing. A book is there forever, but this is a version and the joyful thing would be to please people who love the book while bringing in a new audience.'

An accomplished screenwriter in his own right, with credits that include *Doctor Who* and *Sherlock*, Mark Gatiss joined the production with huge respect for the *Good Omens* co-author, screenwriter and showrunner.

'Neil Gaiman is the laureate of the dispossessed. His work occupies a very special place in the hearts of slightly odd teenagers and wonderfully maladjusted people. He's their patron saint and a legendary writer,' Mark claims, before an air of dry mischief comes into his voice. 'In fact, I wasn't even sure that he existed until I met him.'

ARMAGEDDON APPROACHES

In which the Four Horsepersons of the Apocalypse prepare to call time on the world.

Anyone who expects the end of the world to be heralded by the sound of galloping hooves and a rising dust cloud on the horizon needs to get real. In Terry and Neil's vision, the great cataclysm has been fundamentally reimagined so it isn't just terrifying, it's also very funny.

For one thing, in keeping with the times, the horsemen from the Holy Bible have become motorbike-riding horsepersons, with women in two of the roles. War is now a fearsome redheaded warrior queen played by Mireille Enos and Yusuf Gatewood's Famine a diabolical doctor. In an age of antibiotics Pestilence has retired to be replaced by the contemporary threat of Pollution played by Lourdes Faberes. Not only are they now independent contractors rather than Satan's employees, the task of delivering the summons for each member of the quartet to kick-start Armageddon has been outsourced to an International Express delivery man.

With the exception of Death, a faceless wraith in a hooded cape played by Jamie Hill, War, Pollution and Famine await their calling in quietly malevolent roles around the world. War kills time as an arms dealer in Africa, Pollution is preparing to quietly pull the plug on board a laden oil tanker, while Famine in his guise as Dr Raven Sable promotes a Stateside diet to die for.

In setting the stage for Armageddon on such a global scale, Neil Gaiman, Douglas Mackinnon and the *Good Omens* cast and crew set out to bring all four horsepersons together without compromise. Our introduction to War and her taste for conflict is a case in point. As she walks into a windswept, sun-scorched African village, locals watch her from the sparse shade afforded by tin-topped

An early illustration of the peaceful African village visited by War. Michael Ralph's production design features three telegraph poles that mirror the Crucifixion scene. Like Aziraphale's bookshop, it's another intricately detailed set that goes up in flames.

shacks. Chickens scratch in the dirt under a peace sign daubed on one of the walls. With her truck broken down en route to an arms deal, we follow her into a bar in search of help. It's a simple sequence but one of the more technically impressive ones of the shoot. For one thing, the entire village is in fact a set, built on scrubland over a sand mine just outside Cape Town.

'We created the whole village,' says production designer Michael Ralph. 'It consists of about ten buildings with a bar in the middle. It's on a desert floor with a single track running through it and telegraph wires strung along three poles. I wanted a big peace sign in there, but it was only after we added it that I learned the guy who originally designed it did so as a warning against nuclear war. So it represents the annihilation of the human race, or the apocalypse. That sign we think of as meaning peace is actually showing us what *not* to do,' he says, clearly delighted by the deeper meaning. 'And it's circular,' he adds, completing the picture.

While the production controlled every possible aspect of the shoot, the weather remained in the hands of the gods. In true *Good Omens* style, the conditions proved demanding but ideal for the scene.

'I just remember being blinded by sand,' says script supervisor Jemima Thomas on the windswept environment. 'Gavin is enormously talented, but that was a challenge and he rose to it.'

Acclaimed for his work on *Wolf Hall* and *Gormenghast*, exploiting light and space with stunning effect, the BAFTA award-winning Gavin Finney has come into his own in helping Neil and Douglas achieve their vision for *Good Omens*.

'We just knew it had to knock the socks off everyone,' the director of photography says simply. 'There is nothing else it looks like but *Good Omens*. It's kind of evolved into that.'

In outlining how he established what is a graceful, grand and balletic visual style, in which a camera might drop down into an African village, for example, and then slice through the wall into a tin shack bar, Gavin refers to an early brief from Douglas.

'Douglas said, "I just never want to stop moving,"' he recounts. 'So there are no static establishing shots. We'll swoop in, sometimes very quickly, because the audience are really sophisticated today. They can swallow a lot of information very quickly. It means we don't have to go wide but travel in. For

The village is host to an array of buildings and stalls, including a tin-topped bar riddled with holes and illuminated by sunbeams, with a peace sign daubed prominently on an exterior wall. 'It's a sign warning against the annihilation of the human race,' Michael Ralph explains.

example, we'll begin in a field and move to a house... a room... a person. If we do that really fast there is a kinetic energy that gives everything a lift.'

Gavin credits the production design in enabling him to draw the viewer into the narrative in this unique and compelling way. 'We're making use of the space, and never just saying, "Here's a street" and "Here's a bookshop" before cutting inside, for example. Instead, we're saying, "Here's a street", and then the camera just glides on through the window and pulls you in. But we're not just showing off moves,' he cautions. 'That is driven by the narrative, and led by the need to focus on a character. We have a great story, and the performances are strong, but it really flies as a picture, and anyone watching this will know it's *Good Omens*.'

In delivering fluid camerawork that appears at times to take wing, Gavin Finney and his team commenced shooting prepared for all eventualities.

'We had to make sure that we always had the right equipment to hand,' he says, and reels off the technical names of cameras, drones and rigs that allowed for all manner of moving shots. With such an array of cameras at his disposal, how did Gavin ensure he had the right tools for the job?

'Every day we have everything ready to go so we don't waste time,' he says, and singles out camera operator Matt Fisher, for pushing the steadycam beyond all expectation. 'Ours has an extra arm that allows the camera to start low and go high, as well as fly over tables and objects. Not everyone can operate it, but Matt is really good, and this has given us another dimension. It's a liberation, and has given Douglas a freedom to move. We also carried with us a fifty-foot crane wherever we went,' he adds. 'Having one of those for a few days on a normal TV show would be quite grand. We had it for the whole shoot.'

As a reflection of the ambitions of Douglas, Neil, Gavin and the crew, every day of the shoot saw a fleet of production vehicles and trailers arrive at a location and effectively transform it into a working hive. The location for the African village is a case in point, in which the *Good Omens* production team transformed a windswept tundra into a set build and a humming media outpost complete with mobile offices, dressing rooms, catering tents and even camels (for the Noah's Ark scene that followed in the shooting schedule).

A Horseperson of the Apocalypse walks into a bar... War leaves behind her broken-down truck and prepares to make her presence known.

'It was huge, and just got bigger,' says Gavin, who speaks with great pride about the work achieved here by cast and crew. 'Fifty days is a long shoot, and this was over one hundred. It's a monster, but we're craftspeople and like doing things well.'

Here, Gavin reveals that he had one camera made specially to film what he considers to be his favourite scene in the series. In Episode Five, prompted by God's musing about the number of angels that can dance on the head of a pin, and just ahead of Hastur and Ligur's possessed disco dancing, we see Aziraphale and a troupe of celestial gentlemen perform a nineteenth-century folk dance called the gavotte. It's performed with deadpan panache by Michael Sheen, and lovingly filmed in flickering black and white. It isn't just the quality of the production that excites Gavin but the technical investment and commitment to authenticity.

'I had an HD digital camera hand-built for that scene which could be hand-cranked like a film camera from 1912,' he explains. 'By turning the handle, I could make it go from one to twenty-five frames per second. It meant I could manually control speed and exposure and give it a natural flutter. There was no

post-processing. It was completely organic, and that's something we've tried to do wherever possible. Even though there is a lot of amazing CGI, if we can get a shot in camera then we will. It's all part of the *Good Omens* reality we're creating,' he says, 'and I can't wait to see it!'

Along with his team, Gavin's enthusiasm matches his mastery behind the lens. Nevertheless, with such lofty ambitions, and a constant drive to keep the story moving visually, how does he know that he's achieved the best shot possible every time?

'Douglas is very experienced, and we all understand that he doesn't want to end up in the cutting room wishing we had done better,' he says, 'so we have a lot of eyes on each shot. It would be a very hard job if I ended the day feeling unsatisfied. If I finish feeling shattered but feeling like I've done some great work then I'm buzzing, and I want to come back. It's intense but amazing fun because every day is so vast and the locations are stunning.'

Gavin Finney's enthusiasm doesn't just spring from the opportunity to explore acrobatic camerawork in TV drama with high production values. He proudly lays claim to the fact that he's a long-time fan of the novel.

Under a beating sun, and with the wind whipping up the dust, filming the village scene just outside Cape Town proved challenging for cast and crew.

'I knew the book and I am a fan of both Neil and Terry,' he says. 'As soon as I saw the project I thought that I would love to do it. Then I saw that Douglas was involved, who I've worked with before a few times. I saw him soon afterwards and said how much I was looking forward to seeing what he would do with it.'

If Gavin was excited about seeing the adaptation, he considers the invitation to come on board to be a dream. 'I literally had to drop everything,' he says. 'I found out one day, and the next I was on a flight to Cape Town to look at locations.'

With the scene set in the windblown African village, and much of the crew working with bandanas tied around their mouths and noses, Gavin sought to orchestrate an ambitious sequence to mark War's arrival.

'We started on the crane,' he says, recalling the moment Mireille Enos walks through the heat haze. 'Then we come down, and the camera operator steps off the crane to follow alongside her. As she walks through the door, the operator goes in via a gap in the frontage designed by Michael Ralph. We follow her right up to the bar, which is dark but for shafts of sunlight coming through the tin roof, and then the camera turns around 180 degrees. It's one continuous shot,' Gavin points out, 'and everything had to be planned.'

'The points of light were fantastic,' says first assistant director Cesco Reidy, speaking about the interior bar scene. 'Gavin had to do a lot of work, but those spots are a strong part of the look of the set, and it isn't often you can do that. You have to be somewhere you can rely on the sun.'

Having sparked conflict wherever she goes, War departs from the village as it goes up in flames. True to Michael Ralph's vision, this is where the burning telegraph poles assume a deeper meaning.

'They resemble the crucifixes,' he says, which is in keeping with his bid to bring visual cohesion across the production and executed with stunning effect.

Next we meet War's colleague, Pollution. Played by Lourdes Faberes, she's working on board an oil tanker from which she quietly creates an environmental disaster when nobody is looking. The impact is huge, of course, as is her star turn on the riverbank when the International Express Man tracks her down with a package that spells really bad news for humanity.

War has left the building. Stunts and explosions mark her exit from the scene, and when the trio of telegraph poles are consumed by flames there's no mistaking her intent.

Pollution considers the poetry of rubbish turning in the current.

The scene is unsettling as it's so tranquil. Shot in Surrey, early one morning, and with the river carefully dressed with detritus, we find Pollution lost in thought as she watches the rubbish turning circles in the slow gliding current. As a study in light, colour and composition, we could be looking at an oil painting. It's just there's something very off about it in view of the toxic waterway. For Lourdes Faberes, it also proved to be one of her more challenging moments.

'I wasn't used to wearing contact lenses, and could hardly see a thing,' she says. 'We had an optician, who could lubricate our eyes with drops, but because the first shots were from an overhead drone it meant everyone had to clear the set. I had a radio under the bench where I was sitting, so I could hear when "Action" was called, but for long periods of time I was alone with my drying eyes.'

Lourdes goes on to reveal that she also had a brush with the paparazzi while filming the riverbank scene. 'We were in the public domain which meant a photographer [from the press] got really close.' Wearing a costume that the crew were keen to keep under wraps, Lourdes found herself quickly hustled from view. 'It was mad,' she says. 'Suddenly someone throws a sheet on top of me and starts walking me to the car!'

The instant tarnishing of Pollution's crown will be added by the VFX team in post-production.

Famine makes his first appearance, celebrating the success of his book: *The D-Plan Diet: Slim Yourself Beautiful – Terminally!* in a top-flight New York restaurant. By contrast, Famine's subsequent scene in Episode Three, in which he receives the package from the International Express Man, takes place in a fast-food joint in Des Moines in the American Midwest, and also filmed on set in Cape Town. For this sequence Douglas Mackinnon and Gavin Finney worked on an ambitious introductory crane shot in which the camera takes us into the kitchen for a subtle visual joke before Famine accepts his calling.

'We had an extra made to look like an old Elvis Presley,' says Cesco Reidy. 'The gag being that Elvis is still alive, but we spent hours trying to get the shot and failing. Then, when we finally achieved it and announced that we were moving onto the next shot, someone noticed that Elvis hadn't been in the kitchen. We discovered that without telling anyone he'd taken himself off to the toilet before the take began, which meant we couldn't use it. As we set up all over again,' Cesco continues, 'someone asked why we were shooting yet another take. One of our camera operatives turned around and replied, "Because Elvis left the building."'

There's a guy who works down the Burger Lord who swears he's...

The fast-food joint where Famine receives a package from the
International Express Man was designed by Michael Ralph to be
pure Americana.

THE FOUR HORSEPERSONS OF THE APOCALYPSE

....

MIREILLE ENOS – *WAR*
YUSUF GATEWOOD – *FAMINE*
LOURDES FABERES – *POLLUTION*
JAMIE HILL – *DEATH*

'Miranda Richardson watched the scene where we walk towards the bunker, and just said, "How cool are you four?" Working together has been so much fun, and we get on like a house on fire,' remembers the spirited Lourdes Faberes who plays Pollution.

 Mireille Enos, who plays flame-haired War in *Good Omens*, is convinced that the quartet of mythical motorbike-riders tasked with unleashing Armageddon is neither good nor bad.

'They're neutral,' she insists. 'They're not evil. And don't forget that Heaven wants to see the end of the world as well.'

Like Pollution and Famine, Mireille's character is defined by her distinct costume colours and unblinking gaze. The trio are quietly menacing – even as they await notification of their call-up to climb into the saddle and fulfil their Doomsday destiny. While Death is an unmistakeable wraith in his hooded cape, and effectively makes his existence known to us all in due course, the ultimate calling of his colleagues isn't immediately apparent.

'All three horsepersons are as human as they can be to begin with,' says Mireille. 'They've been hanging out with people and then there's a progression. So by the end they're celestial beings that act more like a four-headed monster than anything attached to the material world.'

On the subject of her character's storyline, Mireille provides a novel interpretation. 'It's a whole hair journey,' she says beaming broadly. 'When we

WAR: No, you listen to me. You may have bought the equipment, but it begins when I get there...

As War puts in a call from a bar in a remote African village, it becomes clear that in her earthly guise she's also an arms dealer.

first meet War, she's in this little scarlet wig, and her hair is shaggy and short. Then we had this idea for a gorgeous Mohawk,' she adds, on describing her ultimate incarnation complete with blood-red eyes. 'That's her battle hair.'

For an actor who plays such a forceful, destructive figure, Mireille Enos is a warm and serene presence. On a break from filming, we've taken refuge from the South African heat, wind and dust to discuss her *Good Omens* experience and the evolution of her character.

'When I said yes to the role I broke out the Book of Revelation,' she says. 'I was reading the passages about the end of the world, and jotted a note to Neil. And he replied, "I'd be careful about reading Revelations. She's more of a cross between Marilyn Monroe and an arms dealer."' Mireille delights in the recollection. 'That was totally my foundation for the character!' she continues. 'War is powerful, while everything is so visual and poignant. It's so delicious when someone says, "Do you want to play War?" Because the answer has to be, "Yes!" And it really has been big fun.'

FAMINE: I've never seen a room full of rich people so hungry.

Only *Good Omens* could make the prospect of playing apocalyptic horsepersons such a blast, but Mireille's experience is echoed by Yusuf Gatewood, who stars as Famine in the series.

'It's hard to highlight a highlight, dude!' declares the Carolina-born American actor on being asked about a favourite moment. 'The opportunity to work with such luminaries is the main thing. These are people I admire so much. I was on set one time and saw Miranda Richardson. I didn't even know she was part of this! And yet everyone is just as kid-like and excited as I am about the project.'

Yusuf's angular cheekbones and mesmerizing gaze makes him ideal to play Dr Raven Sable, Famine's pre-apocalyptic guise and the man responsible for a revolutionary new diet that effectively causes death by starvation. On screen, his appearance is made all the more striking by the addition of a corset under his clothing.

'It changes my posture,' he says, breathing in to demonstrate the effect. 'I was terrified when Claire first showed it to me as it's tight and restricting. But then it forced me to be rigid and upright.' Somewhat surprisingly, Yusuf

Like War, in her role as an arms dealer and reporter, Famine's Dr Raven Sable persona hints at his true identity. This slow reveal is also used to shed light on how Pollution kills time before they're summoned to start the end of the world. As for Death, he's always busy.

Pulling the plug.
Pollution makes her
first appearance on
board a soon-to-be-
less-than-laden
oil tanker.

references Captain Peacock from the classic British seventies sitcom, *Are You Being Served?* as a central influence on his character. 'I grew up in a very small town watching BBC shows,' he explains. 'I loved comedies like *One Foot in the Grave, Fawlty Towers* and *Red Dwarf*. Then, when I was about thirteen, we got cable and, well...' Yusuf Gatewood shrugs and laughs. Whatever turned his attention from there on out – and he offers Neil's novel *American Gods* as a central influence – it's clear his formative years shaped what is a very British sense of humour.

Yusuf also notes that on reading the scripts for *Good Omens*, he saw parallels between the central theme and his own background.

'I'm from the Bible Belt, where everything really was very specifically interpreted as being good or evil. So to have someone like Neil take a comedic turn on that has been fun. He's also been a great resource to have on set, but what I love about him and Douglas is that while they can be specific they're both open to ideas about bringing stuff into the character. Douglas told me that Famine is my guy and that I should make it my own,' says Yusuf, whose performance in *Good Omens* is coolly compelling. 'It's been a blessing working with two people who have earned their stripes but still allow you to do your own thing like that as an actor.'

Like Yusuf Gatewood and Mireille Enos, Lourdes Faberes is thrilled to play one of the key harbingers of doom in the *Good Omens* narrative. As Pollution, and a horseperson for our times, she delivers in spectacular style.

'My character is very capable,' says Lourdes, who has previously worked with Douglas Mackinnon on *Knightfall*. 'What also struck me is that like pollution itself I play an incremental presence. It creeps up on you rather than arriving on your doorstep in one big mound of rubbish. It's insidious and invisible. War is raging and fiery. Famine is striking and in your face in a way that starvation is not easy to ignore. They're both quite zealot, while in my mind Pollution is the one you wouldn't notice to begin with.'

In seeking to understand Pollution's motivation, and get to grips with the scripts, Lourdes took herself to the Netherlands. 'I stayed in a kind of seaside backwater with lots of riverbanks,' she says. 'And that gave me a key to the character, which is based on the idea that we don't care enough. It happens because we drop our rubbish even though there's a bin a hundred metres away, for example. So, my character puts the blame on humans, and has an artist's way of seeing things. Pollution is quite soulful,' she adds, 'and can appreciate beauty in ugly things like the way detritus swirls in water.'

In early drafts of the script, during the casting stage, Neil presented Pollution as male. So it came as a surprise to Lourdes when Douglas invited her to audition.

'He just told me to be bold with it,' she says. Having played the role of an assassin masquerading as a man in *Knightfall*, and with the script in mind, Lourdes Faberes pursued an androgynous look while streaking her hair with strands of white. Having struck the right note for Douglas Mackinnon, she explains how Pollution's gender remained fluid throughout the costume and make-up phase of pre-production.

'We decided not to emphasize it one way or the other,' she says. 'Not too masculine and not too feminine. The character isn't human anyway. We didn't think about it, and just focused on the look. So Pollution has ice-blue eyes,

Costume designer, Claire Anderson was looking for the 'essence of a character' in her dressing of the Four Horsepersons. Strong colours are key here, along with individual twists such as Famine's corset to cinch his waist, War's warrior hairstyle and Pollution's grubby, soiled clothing. When it comes to Death, the colour black speaks volumes.

which works so well with the blonde hair, and those eyes become oily black as the apocalypse approaches.'

Fittingly for her role as a horseperson of the apocalypse, Lourdes Faberes is a force of nature. She's passionate about her profession and speaks of her experience on *Good Omens* with a sense of joy and also awe at working with such an illustrious cast. 'To do this for a living has been so much fun!' she says, and goes on to reveal that she's formed a close bond with her fellow riders. 'They're wonderful. We get on really well, and even text each other using four motorbike emojis.'

As the final member of the foursome tasked with ending the world, Death stands out from his colleagues in more ways than one. A skeleton in a hooded robe from the moment we meet him, there's no human guise for this horseperson before the International Express Man tracks him down with a package in his name. Death is also ominously tall, which is down to the actor who breathes life into this emperor of the End Times, Jamie Hill.

'Monsters are my thing,' says Jamie, who stands at six foot five and has made regular appearances as different beasts in *Doctor Who*. He credits his height, in fact, for first coming to the attention of a TV producer behind the long-running series. 'I have no acting background,' he confesses. 'I was studying business studies and marketing, and was late for a lecture. I just happened to be outside at the right time.'

Jamie Hill is a warm, relaxed and friendly presence. He talks humbly about his pathway to *Good Omens* and with touching honesty when he discusses his relationship with acting.

'It's tricky!' he says, before admitting to a degree of shyness and sensitivity that would persuade most people to stay away from stage and screen. 'I go bright red very easily, but playing monsters means I have a mask on, and that's when I feel a lot more confident.'

To illustrate the challenge, Jamie tells the story of his experience appearing in a *Doctor Who* stage spectacular.

'The cast had to rehearse in front of each other out of costume, but I just couldn't do it,' he says. 'I could feel my face had gone bright red. So the

Road to Hell. At an unassuming roadside café, the Four Horsepersons assemble ahead of Armageddon.

movement choreographer gave me a mask and it transformed me. I hit every mark and got a round of applause at the end.' Jamie is aware of what it is about covering his face and head that enables him to play the role required. 'It helps me to feel closed off in my own world. I'm looking inward rather than outward, and can't see the people looking at me.'

In filming *Good Omens*, Jamie Hill's mask is effectively a canvas for visual effects supervisor JC Deguara and his team at Milk VFX.

'My face is going to be a skull,' Jamie explains. 'So I wear the death robes, or the biker outfit when I'm on the motorbike, and a kind of green Lycra hood. The visual effects people put markers on so they know where my nose and mouth is, which is fine. I'm used to not having any vision and stuff.'

Even before the addition of the skull, and the voice provided by Emmy-Award-winning actor Brian Cox, Jamie Hill's Death is a commanding presence.

'I can still be in character when we're not filming,' he says. 'One time I was crouching down near the kids who play the Them. Then I rose up to my full height, with a mask and robes on, and I could sense their freaked-out vibe.'

Nobody escapes Death, as everyone knows, and Jamie Hill's ominous

As the end of the world draws closer, War, Pollution and Famine evolve from human form and take on otherworldly qualities while Death swaps his biker's helmet for the dreaded hood.

character is impossible to ignore. Together with his fellow horsepersons, he casts a shadow across *Good Omens* that chills and thrills in equal measure.

The Four Horsepersons are by turns both menacing and oddly endearing. However, those familiar with the novel will no doubt register the absence of the Four Other Riders of the Apocalypse who they encounter in a rundown café as they close in on Tadfield. The meeting of the two groups is a comic masterclass, as is the untimely death of all but one of the Other Riders shortly afterwards in a motorway pile up involving a heap of fish. While it's a favourite scene for many fans of the book, Neil Gaiman, is candid about his reason for keeping them off the road and screen in the TV adaptation.

'Terry died and left me, and this was his last request,' he says. 'My job is to make this something he would be proud of, and sometimes that meant I'm more likely to hold my position on a thing that Terry wrote than something I wrote. In this case, I was willing to lose the four other horsemen from the script, a week before shooting, for budgetary reasons. I looked at the script and thought I can pull it out and it does no harm. Even though some people will be disappointed, my response is that it's still in the book.'

Famine comes face to face with his junior counterpart, Wensleydale, and looks like he'll have the lad for breakfast.

THE INTERNATIONAL EXPRESS MAN

SIMON MERRELLS

'He's the best delivery man in the world. He loves his job, and he's fantastic at it. That's why he's been chosen, but he doesn't know he's been chosen.'

Simon Merrells recounts Douglas Mackinnon's take on his character by adopting the director's strong Scottish accent. He's very good at voices, and one of those actors who can effortlessly switch in and out of them as he reflects on the fun he's had playing the individual charged with delivering the badges of office to the Four Horsepersons of the Apocalypse.

'It's an utter departure from the stuff I've been doing in recent years,' says the amiable and engaging British actor best known for playing Marcus Licinius Crassus in *Spartacus: War of the Damned*. 'I'm always cast in armour on a horse, and I love doing that, but I'm so grateful to Douglas for giving me the chance to explore this gentle soul.'

Travelling to the four corners of the earth to deliver special packages without questioning the contents, the International Express Man is a charmingly enigmatic individual. Simon says it was this characterization along with the pedigree of the scripts that convinced him to take on the role.

'I was in LA at the time, and my agent is a big Terry Pratchett fan. She said, "Don't just skim to your part. You have to read the whole thing!" So I settled myself down to slog through all the scripts, and I was just gripped from the beginning,' he says, confessing to bursts of laughter throughout. 'I was amazed by the originality and the inventiveness of the humour,' he continues. 'As for my part, I just thought the guy was delightful. He's aware that something strange is going on, but his main priority is to do his job well and get back to his

The International
Express Man finally
finds War in the midst
of disrupting a
press conference.

wife, whom he loves. It's Shakespearean really, in which you have great scenes with history and nobles and then a moment with a gatekeeper talking about life. I read Neil's script and thought, "Why did you do that, you crazy genius?" Is it pushing forward the story? Not really, but it's making it richer,' he says, echoing Neil's commitment to the set-up. 'Everything in this piece has been arranged and organized for the lead-up to Armageddon,' Simon continues. 'So, he's a tiny cog, but an important cog, and you have to take the view in this story that he's been chosen because he's trustworthy.'

Simon Merrells goes on to explain why he opted for a light touch in his portrayal of the character who travels around the world to present Famine, Pollution, War and Death with packaged tokens that engage them to bring on the Apocalypse.

'I've tried to play him with restraint,' he says. 'I hope my instincts have been right with it, but any time you push too hard in any direction it doesn't feel right. With this guy, he's just open-faced and honest. It's what you see in this extraordinary tale, and I tried to do it... gently,' he adds after a brief pause for reflection.

Claire Anderson designed a modern, utilitarian costume for the International Express Man that is recognisable the world over.

Man with a van. Simon Merrill's uncomplaining character travels around the world delivering the packages to the Four Horsepersons that will ultimately trigger Armageddon.

INTERNATIONAL EXPRESS MAN:
Red sky in the morning,
shepherd's warning. Or is it
sailor's warning?

Fired up by the role and under the guidance of Douglas and Neil, how did Simon find the shoot itself?

'I felt pretty nervy about it,' he confesses. 'Yes, it's a small role but it's in a show full of top-notch people with the best scripts I've ever read. I feel a responsibility with any part I do, but in this case, I wanted to get the tone right. I know Douglas would've pushed me in another direction if needs be,' he says, 'but I heard my character's voice early on, and it's been great.'

In conversation with the affable actor, it's clear that he's enjoyed the entire process in his role as the trustworthy courier who doesn't question what each package contains even when faced with Death. One highlight, he says, was the opportunity to work with Indra Ové, who plays his screen wife.

'We met a few seconds before we started working and then suddenly we're in love,' laughs Simon, whose contribution to *Good Omens* is as quietly melancholic as it is memorable. 'It's been a real pleasure,' he reports happily. 'A joyous piece of work and a change for me from being psychopathic knights, Templar heroes or Roman generals.'

On the banks of a polluted river, shot just outside Guildford in Surrey, the International Express Man ticks another off the list.

THE BENTLEY AND BEYOND

In which we find out how to film on wheels and not destroy a priceless motor.

If there's one thing that Crowley treasures in this world more than anything else – even Aziraphale himself – it's his car. Since publication of the novel, *Good Omens* readers have come to consider Crowley's 1926 black Bentley as a character in its own right. Leave any tape in the car's stereo and within weeks it'll morph into *The Best of Queen*, while it's capable of travelling at eye-watering speeds that perhaps only a demon driver can handle. Thanks to the creative glee of Terry Pratchett and Neil Gaiman, Crowley also floors the accelerator with the car on fire.

Much is left to the imagination on the page, but how does such a key (and fast-moving) component of the *Good Omens* world translate to the screen? Throw Madame Tracy's flying scooter into the mix, along with Newt's iconic Japanese Wasabi car (dubbed Dick Turpin), Mr Young's Morris Traveller and the four horsepersons' customized chrome chargers – as well as setting a gridlocked major UK orbital motorway ablaze – and it's clear that such diverse and often fantastical vehicle sequences would present Douglas Mackinnon and crew with a series of significant technical challenges.

Script supervisor Jemima Thomas regards the *Good Omens* Bentley as more than just a vintage car.

'Aziraphale has his bookshop, and I know Crowley has a flat, but in some ways the Bentley is more of a home to him. He loves it like a child.'

With several scenes taking place inside the car, and not just on fire or at speed, director of photography Gavin Finney was determined to create an air of authenticity that went above and beyond a conventional shoot with a vehicle

Valued at £250,000, the Bentley used through filming was handled with great care and reverence.

While Douglas was committed to capturing as much footage 'on camera' without resorting purely to visual effects, Madame Tracy's flying scooter required some post-production work in order to look wholly convincing.

centre stage. A case in point is the collision on a country lane in Episode Two. From the moment the demon behind the wheel slams on the brakes in vain, we feel the thud just as he does and empathize with Aziraphale in the passenger seat as his face falls. By the time the angel has helped to pick Anathema and her bicycle out of the ditch, while Crowley magically attends to a dent in the Bentley, it really does feel like a fully-fledged road accident.

'Interior car shots are often unsatisfactory,' says Gavin, and offers the example of how shooting a scene and then using visual effects to stitch in footage of the view from the vehicle's windows means the actor behind the wheel isn't seen to be reacting realistically to every turn, bump or jolt.

The solution, according to Gavin, was to bring an old technique up to date. 'We used a form of back projection,' he says, and explains a process that begins with filming passing scenery from the sides, front and rear of a moving car. On set, the footage is then projected on to a screen surrounding the stationary vehicle. 'It means you see the footage as well as reflections on the glass or the driver's face, say as the vehicle goes under trees, while it also works as a lighting source,' he adds. 'You never get this from using a green screen because

Aziraphale has his bookshop – a precious retreat from the world around – and Crowley has his Bentley.

A replica shell of the
Bentley was used for
scenes demanding
close camerawork
inside the vehicle, or
when using the real
thing risked anything
from a scratch to
the paintwork to its
outright destruction.

the lighting isn't real and this way the actor can see where they're supposed to be and react to it.

'As a technique,' he continues, 'it's completely interactive, and means we can shoot the Bentley apparently travelling at 120 mph or play with flame effects. So we have a real Bentley, a CGI Bentley and a model Bentley. Along with plates and back projection, this means we can have shots where we'll start outside the vehicle, driving fast, and then the camera will appear to go in through the side window, turn and then look out of the front window. Almost every shot involves multiple disciplines to create what will be exciting moves for the audience and "How did they do that?" moments.' One other driving factor in filming the Bentley came down to the rarity of the vehicle itself. With an accurate model at their disposal, and one careful owner on set to watch over proceedings, it fell to Douglas Mackinnon to secure the footage he needed without putting a scratch in the real car's paintwork. On screen, Crowley might be able to repair any damage at the flick of a finger. In reality, this wasn't an option, and yet the fact remained that in Neil's script the Bentley meets an explosive end.

'We used a genuine Bentley shell for the model,' explains special effects supervisor Danny Hargreaves. 'Even that was really expensive, as the car is so rare, and so we only had one shot at blowing it up and the pressure was on! When we were rigging it,' he continues, 'the guy who owns the original vehicle was eyeing it up. I could tell that what we were about to do to it was breaking his heart. At one point, he asked, "Are you really blowing this up?" And I replied, "It's either yours or this, so what would you rather?"'

Inside the director's tent, with just one available attempt to get it right, script supervisor Jemima Thomas explains why it had to be done for real.

'This is *Good Omens*,' she says. 'If something is going to blow up or burn down then it has to be for real. Douglas is adamant that if this is what happens in the script then it's what we need to see, and I love that about him,' she adds.

UK producer Phil Collinson regards the focus on authenticity to be an engine of invention throughout the *Good Omens* shoot.

'Sometimes with an unlimited budget you don't have to think,' he says. 'With *Good Omens* we have to think on our feet and that's when it becomes a creative environment. Take Madame Tracy's scooter, which she rides high up in the air.

Crowley takes Hastur on a ride from Hell.

We could've done this with VFX, but following discussions we decided it was funnier if it was just above ground. There are camera tricks we can play to achieve that while making it look and feel better.'

If filming such ambitious vehicle scenes proved this taxing for the *Good Omens* crew, perhaps their greatest challenge lay in adapting the novel's celebrated and apocalyptic M25 Ring of Fire scene. In keeping with the scale of the End Times, Terry Pratchett and Neil Gaiman had torched London's orbital ring road at a keystroke. How did they fare in summoning such an epic moment for the screen?

'That was the one I couldn't get my head around,' admits first assistant director Cesco Reidy. 'It felt as if we would have to close down a section of two motorways, and I just didn't see anyone giving us permission to do this. It wasn't that I didn't know *how* we would shoot it,' he explains, 'but *where*. So, all credit to Nick Marshall for finding it.

Gloucestershire's Moreton-in-Marsh, thirty miles north-west of Oxford, is home to the Fire Service College. The facility includes an impressive 300-acre 'incident ground'. Here, in what is effectively a purpose-built disaster

The green tape on this vintage Bentley will be transformed in post-production to flames and smoke.

Crowley's beloved Bentley meets a fiery end at the airbase, and yet as the owner is a demon there's every chance it'll come back from the dead.

playground, emergency service professionals are trained in tackling major incidents such as train derailments, building blazes and aircraft crashes. As location manager Nick Marshall discovered on a recce for *Good Omens*, the site also includes a faithful replica of a four-lane motorway section known as the M96.

'It's 400 yards long,' he says. 'We knew that we could extend the length with visual effects, but this gave us the potential for scale.'

On visiting the location, UK producer Phil Collinson says the question mark that had hovered over the scene was removed at a stroke.

'With one hundred extras in their cars, and wind and rain thanks to the special effects guys, we were able to put together a huge motorway jam. We then created a curtain of flames by shooting through fire bars and achieved the sense of scale we needed that we could never have done on the actual M25.'

With cars, bikes, scooters and burning thoroughfares in the can, Douglas Mackinnon and his crew turned their attention to a vehicle that Neil's script had summoned from another planet. As Adam Young wakes up to the fact that he's in possession of extraordinary and potentially infernal powers, so he finds that ideas in his mind take shape in reality. The UFO that Jack Whitehall's Newt encounters on a lane outside Tadfield is a case in point. Here, Douglas had a specific vision in terms of handling what is effectively the product of a child's imagination.

'In *Good Omens*, I was very keen on creating a coherent difference between the work of the angels, God and the stuff that the human do,' he begins. 'Aziraphale and Crowley are very casual about their magic, for example. They know the vocabulary and can do it with a tiny little finger movement, whereas Adam's magic is based on his experience in life. So the flying saucer isn't a state-of-the-art craft from *Star Wars* but how a child might picture it, and we based ours on one built by my eleven-year-old daughter out of cardboard.'

Cesco Reidy acknowledges that while the creative tools exist on set and in post-production to create a sleek and sophisticated spacecraft, Douglas's approach contributes to the distinct *Good Omens* vibe.

'It's where our story gets its charm,' he says simply.

When Adam imagines a UFO, the dream becomes a reality thanks to his emerging powers as the Antichrist. Here, Douglas and Neil were keen to create the kind of saucer an eleven-year-old boy might make from household items. For the sake of authenticity, Douglas used a model constructed by his young daughter as the basis for the craft.

A SATANIC SHOWDOWN

In which we witness the moment of truth and a Bentley blown to Kingdom Come.

In asking every member of the *Good Omens* cast and crew to nominate a notable moment in the production, almost all of them flag up the shoot for the climactic scene in the series. Many will say how memorable it was to see so many stellar actors of their generation assemble for what is the moment in both the novel and the adaptation when the countdown to the apocalypse approaches the final tick. Here, the four horsepersons descend on an airbase just outside Tadfield and then sweep into its communications centre. In a world so closely interconnected by technology, they plan to unleash havoc around the world at the touch of a button. With War intent on punching in the nuclear codes, Pollution envisaging the chemical fall out that follows and Famine looking forward to fatal food shortages, there's something in it for all them – but most of all for Death.

'This is *Good Omens*,' says the director of photography Gavin Finney, about a shoot that refused to compromise. 'In the book, the scene is set on a major US airbase in England. So, we went and found a massive US airbase in England.'

With representatives of good and evil in a face off, as well as those humans swept up in a bid to save the world, the gathering featured everyone from David Tennant and Michael Sheen to Adria Arjona, Jack Whitehall, Jon Hamm, Miranda Richardson, Michael McKean, Daniel Mays and Anna Maxwell Martin, as well as the ensembles playing the four horsepersons and the Them. But while the assembly was remarkable for its pedigree of stars, what made this particular shoot stand out for so many was the biting cold.

'It's a huge flat plain,' Gavin points out about the airbase location, which is now RAF Upper Heyford, in Oxfordshire. 'And we were shooting in the middle of winter.'

RAF Upper Heyford in Oxfordshire proved to be the perfect location to host a face-off between the forces of darkness and light as Michael Ralph showed in his production designs.

U.S. AIRFORCE
AIR BASE
WARNING
U.S. AIRFORCE PROPERTY
AUTHORIZED PERSONNEL ONLY
100% ID CHECK
IN PROGRESS
DEADLY FORCE WILL BE USED

'Deep, deep down,' says Jack Whitehall, 'beneath the freezing depths, I did enjoy filming that scene. It took us days, with twenty pages of dialogue, but to be working with all those people was so exciting.'

'The days on that airstrip were bleak, cold and numbing,' agrees Michael McKean. 'But I also got to spend a lot of time in a nice, warm trailer with David, Michael, Adria, Miranda, Jon, Jack and Anna, and we had such a nice time.'

While the freezing conditions proved testing for everyone, the crew were presented with the problem of ensuring the location looked consistent across the shoot.

'Sometimes we had to start and finish the same scene with days in between,' says Cesco Reidy. 'This is difficult as the weather can change, and we've got no control over that, and we wanted to avoid shooting in the dry one day and find it's raining the next. So Douglas came up with a solution, which involved wetting down the entire tarmac apron of the airbase. It meant before each shoot we had massive fire engines driving up and down with sprinkler systems.'

For Mireille Enos, the airbase scene served as yet another reminder that she was contributing to a production that sought to achieve as much as possible

... only to come face to face with the Four Horsepersons of the Apocalypse astride their steel steeds.

in camera. Having arrived alongside her colleagues on formidable motorbikes, War, together with Famine, Pollution and Death, are empowered to instigate the end of the world by the biblical tokens that have been hand-delivered to each of them by the International Express Man. For War, this means brandishing the flaming sword that Aziraphale handed to Adam at the dawn of time.

'All the way through filming there was talk that the flaming sword was coming,' says Mireille. 'I assumed it would just be the hilt, and that the flaming sword itself would be added as CGI. Instead, on the airstrip, I discover it's an *actual* sword, wrapped in rope, dipped in a combustible fluid and on fire. So, I'm supposed to manipulate it,' she says, reliving the moves by swishing the air, 'and yet I couldn't help thinking that I was also wearing a big red wig covered in hair spray...' She tails off there and mimics an explosion. 'It was a little terrifying, but so much fun.'

Despite challenging conditions, Douglas Mackinnon delivers a spectacular showdown in which Satan himself makes an appearance, if not in person then at least in the VFX added by JC Deguara's team at Milk. It's reminiscent of a Western in its face-off between good and evil, and a thriller when personnel on

Mireille Enos gets to grips with Aziraphale's visual-effects-free flaming sword.

a Russian submarine and US missile silos receive instructions to prepare for war – while retaining a touchingly domestic comic edge when Adam's dad rides in to the rescue in his Morris Traveller.

Above all, Douglas remains committed to telling the story of *Good Omens* in a unique visual language. It's one that never sacrifices authenticity on the altar of visual effects, while ensuring that any wizardry is embedded in the frame rather than dominating it. According to script supervisor Jemima Thomas, this approach has enabled Douglas to capture large-scale, real-life scenes throughout the series and render them out of this world.

'He doesn't do anything by halves,' she says. '*Good Omens* is epic in scale and he has been absolutely committed to sticking with that idea. We did everything as big and as best as we could. And we all enjoyed it so much. I've worked on big productions but this will stay with me. It's been magical and crazy and unlike anything else.'

Several weeks after the final day of shooting, I visit Douglas Mackinnon in a London post-production suite as he prepares to embark upon the first phase of the editing process. For a man who has steered a gargantuan production through

Filming on the airbase across several days, with variable weather conditions, persuaded Douglas to hire a fire truck to wet down the tarmac before each shoot and maintain a consistent look. Here, the Them face up to the fact that Armageddon is a very big deal indeed.

With Satan's appearance conjured in post-production, and voiced by *Sherlock* and *Avengers* star Benedict Cumberbatch, the principal cast were required to act in an imaginary shadow of evil in order to provide Douglas with the raw footage required. In a climax that sees the world upon the brink of destruction, Douglas set out to achieve a vision that incorporated live action with visual effects in one seamless sequence.

a schedule that would leave many directors with a thousand-yard stare, he looks remarkably fresh and as enthusiastic as ever. Along with banks of footage, with each take carefully documented by script supervisor Jemima Thomas, Douglas also keeps his annotated copy of *Good Omens* close at hand. This might be an adaptation optimized for a television audience, but the director is committed to realizing the spirit and vision of the book's co-authors as closely as possible. In a few days' time, Neil is set to fly in from the USA and join the director in crafting a six-part comic fantasy drama that spans millennia, makes insightful comments about the nature of good and evil and looks like nothing else. How does he feel at this stage in translating *Good Omens* from page to screen?

'It has its own energy that is way bigger than me or Neil, and it comes alive in front of you,' he says, surrounded by the banks of screens and wizardry that furnish this state-of-the-art cutting room. 'While everything blooms from the script, it can't be a finished thing because that's what we're doing.

Douglas Mackinnon falls silent for a moment as if to consider the enormity of this undertaking. Then he draws breath, and I can almost see the vision in his eyes. 'It's the beginning,' he adds simply.

A common purpose? The angel and the demon face the possibility of Armageddon.

END TIMES

In which Terry Pratchett's representative in this world reflects on the devil of a job well done.

'Neil has done a fantastic job of adapting *Good Omens* while keeping Terry's soul in it, and I respect him for that.'

Rob Wilkins is a man of many roles. Fans of the late Sir Terry Pratchett will know him as the fantasy novelist's loyal personal assistant; the creative sounding board who also dealt with the day-to-day business and administrative dealings that might otherwise have distracted Terry from his prolific output. In the author's final years, following his diagnosis with Alzheimer's disease, Rob's ever-present and gentle support enabled Terry to write and complete seven additional bestsellers. Since the author's death in March 2015, Rob's role has evolved to steer and manage Terry's literary estate while keeping his memory vividly alive. In the words of Neil Gaiman himself, Rob Wilkins is doing a fine job as 'Terry's representative on Earth'.

Now immersed in the world of Narrativia, an independent production company set up to manage multimedia Terry Pratchett projects, Rob Wilkins serves as an executive producer on *Good Omens*. In some ways, with his old boss absent, he regards his involvement as a means of keeping the torch burning brightly, and ensuring that the prolific work of a master fantasy writer lives on through future generations.

'We have the visual references like Terry's hat and his novels in Aziraphale's bookshop. They're in it to remind us, but there's more than that,' he says on a bracingly cold day in a green room with me at West London Film Studios. Over on set, just behind Douglas and his monitors, sit two high canvas chairs. One has Neil Gaiman's name on the back and the other has Rob's. 'Neil says he needed to be involved because of Terry, and so do I. We're channelling Terry so people know he's there.'

Formerly assistant to Terry Pratchett and now one of *Good Omens* executive producers, Rob Wilkins has played a key role in the story of the adaptation from script to screen.

Rob Wilkins speaks with great sincerity as a friend of the late author and as a disciple of his books as well as in his role as executive producer. At times, I can't be certain in what capacity he's speaking, but his loyalty is fierce across them all. 'I can't think of any member of the crew who would've worked with Terry, or met him, and yet they have all picked up on his character and his way of doing things,' he says. 'They know they've got to make it the best they can for him.'

To illustrate his point, Rob refers to an earlier observation he'd made on set. 'Our props guy was outside making a little leather writing set for Aziraphale. He was standing outside in the cold, wearing fingerless gloves and using a knife to furnish this beautiful thing. It will probably get two seconds of screen time, and I watched and thought to myself, "That's it. That's Terry right there!" He'd have put as much detail into the writing, and it may not even be noticed, but the story would have been poorer without it.' 'Take Agnes Nutter's witch's roll,' he continues, 'Michael Ralph opened it up and made sure that tool and herb had a reason for being there, which is a lovely touch. Then there's Crowley's watch, which contains little gears with belts. It's such a beautiful thing, and Terry would've been quite happy if you have to watch the series two or three times to start picking up the different levels, but even that probably isn't enough.' Rob lets the observation hang in the air for a moment. '*Good Omens* was Neil's original idea, but then it took the soul of Terry, the fantastic storytelling ability that only he could do. It wasn't even second nature to Terry. It was *first* nature, and more important than eating, sleeping or drinking, and together they wrote a wonderful tale. *Good Omens* has sold millions of copies since it was published, but for a long time it was a mystery about how to get it on the screen. Now Neil has done it,' declares Rob with genuine excitement. 'I reserve the word genius for very few people, but Neil is one of them. He's got that genius.'

Rob Wilkins worked at Sir Terry Pratchett's side from 1998. He witnessed at first hand the significant hurdles and milestones that Terry and Neil faced in adapting the novel for the screen. After the pair recognized that film was no longer the right platform, alongside the rise of long-form TV drama, Rob recounts how they arranged to meet to discuss the way forward.

'Neil was working on his first *Doctor Who* in Cardiff,' he says. 'So we drove over from Terry's home in Salisbury, which is a big deal for Terry as normally people came to see him. But this is Neil. He'd come over from the USA, put out on Twitter if anyone knew of a good sushi restaurant, and had been deluged with suggestions. So Terry and I met Neil along with Rod Brown. Rod was interested in adapting *Good Omens*, and in fact he would go on to become part of Narrativia. Together with Rod, we sat down and ate sushi, and it was very nice. Neil and Terry hadn't seen each other for some time. Both had just been really busy and doing incredibly well, and as they talked all the years between them evaporated. They had arrived as two people who were very different than when they wrote *Good Omens*, but very quickly the anecdotes began flying across the table. You could see the electricity between them, and when it came to making a decision about the adaptation they sent Rod out to have a cigarette. Before he'd even walked out of the door they'd agreed between themselves to go with him, but because it was a horrible, rainy night they felt it would be more fun to leave him out there for a while. Having watched Rod smoke his way through two cigarettes before bringing him back in, we ordered champagne and posed for a

Men in black: Rob, Neil and Terry at Terry's home in Wiltshire.

photograph to mark the occasion. In short, that was the moment that Neil and Terry agreed that a TV adaptation was the way forward.'

Such is Rob Wilkins' passion and commitment to the life and work of Terry Pratchett that he can account for every detail of all the novels and projects that the fantasy writer worked on throughout their time together. He explains that, like Neil, Terry was just too busy to write the script for *Good Omens*. With the BBC in the frame, the pair had been happy to leave the adaptation process in the hands of another writer. Then, he says, everything changed following Terry's diagnosis with Alzheimer's and the unsparing decline that followed.

'In the autumn of 2014, Neil came over from America to see Terry at his house. I sat them in the library. Now, Terry was finding it quite difficult. He struggled to follow conversations, but with Neil he brightened up. I said I'd pop out and find some lunch. It seemed appropriate to leave these two old friends together, and I left them singing songs.' During this time, Rob reports, Neil and Terry also spoke about Neil writing the adaptation of *Good Omens*. 'When I came back, we ate scampi together and then I drove Neil to the train station. It turned out to be the final time they saw each other.'

Rob attends the *Good Omens* read-through with an appropriately symbolic apple beside his script. By his own admission, Rob is often tempted by 'narrative lust' at a read-through, in which he struggles not to lose himself to the pleasure of the story instead of focusing on content, form and structure.

Rob Wilkins still finds it hard to talk about Sir Terry's death in March 2015. At the same time, he recognizes that everyone processes grief in different ways. For Neil Gaiman, he believes, the loss prompted an undertaking to honour his late friend's last wish.

'Neil started writing the adaptation in the weeks after Terry died. He came over for the funeral, and must have begun work on it immediately afterwards. In doing that so soon after Terry left us, I feel it meant his presence is embedded in Neil's scripts.'

If Rob is thrilled by the shape and substance of Neil's adaptation, his delight at the *Good Omens* production draws an enthusiastic smile that stays with him as he talks through his early experience of the process.

'At the read-through, I asked David Tennant if he and Michael Sheen had worked together before. He said no, but that in twenty minutes' time they'd know what music they could make together.' Judging by Rob's expression, the outcome was symphonic. 'A read-through is like my own personal performance,' continues the experienced executive producer. 'I close my eyes and I can shoot it in my mind. But then because I'm caught up in the narrative lust I find it really

Rob and Neil on set and in their hot seats.

difficult to see how it's going to be made from a practical filmmaking point of view. At the *Good Omens* read-through, however, I looked around and saw other people's reactions and I thought, "Bloody hell, this works!"'

As well as managing other Pratchett projects, Rob has been a regular presence on the *Good Omens* set.

'Unlike books, making TV is a slow process,' he observes, speaking as someone who worked closely with a novelist who was known for his prolific output. 'But then everyone here is happy with the pace and you have to realize it's just a completely different medium. It's also an ambitious production and Douglas is incredible. His timekeeping is so consistent, and when you see the story take shape you know it's never going to take its foot off the gas.'

In considering what lies at the heart of *Good Omens* as a story, Rob Wilkins draws breath as if he's about to share a password that opens a vault of treasure.

'It's clever,' he says quite simply. 'The funny is the dollop on top. I read it years ago on a train, and had to process what I'd just read because it was so smart. Funny doesn't do it justice. Fast forward to my job sitting next to Terry at the word processor. If he wrote something that worked I'd jump out of my seat in delight. Then I'd go out to put the kettle on, and when I came back with the tea Terry would be sitting there grinning with his arms folded. Why?' he asks. 'Because he'd tweaked it just a little more and made it better. For Terry, it was about making something funny and then trying that little bit harder. So for me, is the adaptation of *Good Omens* about the comedy? Well, sometimes it's funny because it's about a demon and angel and the situation they're in, but it's also very serious about the possibility of Armageddon. We're not talking about a metaphor. It's actually about the world coming to an end.' Rob Wilkins is used to addressing what his old friend would have made of the adaptation, and answers with complete confidence.

'He'd have been overjoyed. That's not what I think but absolutely what I know. He'd be overjoyed at the casting, the costumes, the hair and make-up, the locations and everyone on board. Neil's script is genius and he has made Terry proud, which is all Terry asked of him, and he has achieved it without compromise. Take the Satanic nuns,' he says, sounding more animated by the moment,

'they are so funny in this, and Neil had wound them up to 'eleven', but they don't go beyond it. There's no need to wind them up to the point of breaking. Had *Good Omens* been the Hollywood version from the early nineties, I think it would've come and gone, and everyone would have been moderately happy. But this is *unique*,' he stresses. 'You can't tell the story properly in one hundred minutes, and here we are with six episodes and all the constraints removed.'

As a man committed to ensuring that Terry Pratchett's star continues to shine brightly, Rob Wilkins knows that the TV adaptation of *Good Omens* will please loyal fans and invite new generations to the great body of work he left behind. For this, his gratitude towards the novel's co-author, scriptwriter and series showrunner is heartfelt.

'Terry would be incredibly upset about being dead, and not being able to see it,' he says. 'I feel cheated on his behalf that he didn't, but we got it right. My God, this is the cornerstone now, and we have Neil Gaiman to thank for that. He was there with Terry at the birth of the novel. In adapting it, his approach has been to say this is how it's written, and this is how we're going to shoot it, and nobody else could've done that.'

After filming on *Good Omens* wrapped, motor enthusiast Rob became the proud owner not only of Famine's bare bones motorcycle but of the bikes ridden by Death, Pollution and war too.

DOUGLAS MACKINNON
DIRECTOR/EXECUTIVE PRODUCER
14mm
DEAD BATT
NEIL GAIMAN
SHOWRUNNER

Over a hundred days of shooting. We've been frozen and broiled, sandstormed and snowed, dogbitten and burned down. We've not had any two days of shooting that were like any other two. Through it all we've persisted, telling a story about Peace vs War, about looking after this world because it's the only one we have, about making the right choices. Thank you, all of you, from Terry Pratchett, and from me.

Neil Gaiman

Thank you everyone for completing this marathon shoot. It is hard to believe that principal photography is now over. 109 days of *Good Omens*. To the UK crew that have seen it through all the days, I'd give you medals and a place in heaven if I could, if it wasn't for the fact that I don't believe in hierarchy or heaven. So, delight at your work will have to do. To the UK crew that didn't come with us, if you're listening, we missed you here. To the SA crew, you have delighted and surprised us on a daily basis. Thank you all!

Douglas xx

Writer and Showrunner
Neil Gaiman

Director and Executive Producer
  Douglas Mackinnon

1st Assistant Director
  Francesco 'Cesco' Reidy

2nd Assistant Director
  Jan Zalar

3rd Assistant Director
  Noel Corbally

Script Supervisor
  Jemima Thomas

Script Editor
  Charlotte Webber

Editor
  Will Oswald

Editor
  Emma Oxley

Assistant Editor
  Cat Gregory

Executive Producers for BBC Studios
    Chris Sussman
    Simon Winstone

Executive Producer for Narrativia
    Rob Wilkins

For Amazon Studios
    Ryan Andolina
    Punit Mattoo
    Gina Kwon

Producers
   Phil Collinson
   Paul Frift
   Tim Bradley
   Josh Dynevor

Head of Production
   Radford Neville

Production Executive
   Eirwen Davies

Co-Producer
   Mike Treen

Line Producer (UK)
   Joanne Crowther

Line Producer (SA)
   Samantha Putter

Production Manager
   Kyla Brennan

Production Coordinator (UK)
   Catherine Booton

Production Co-ordinator (SA)
   Nomfundo Mabaso

Director of Photography
  Gavin Finney

Camera and Steadicam Operator/
Augmented Reality Operator
  Matt Fisher

Camera and Steadicam Operator (SA)
  Vince McGahon

Camera Operator (UK)
  Ed Clark

Lighting Gaffer
  Andy Bailey

Lighting Gaffer (SA)
  Lesley Manuel

Key Grip (UK)
  Rupert Lloyd Parry

Key Grip (SA)
  Mark Davidson

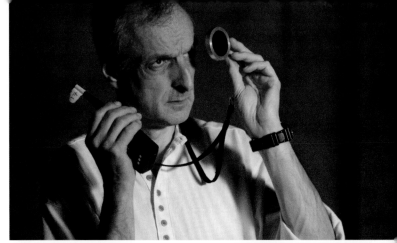

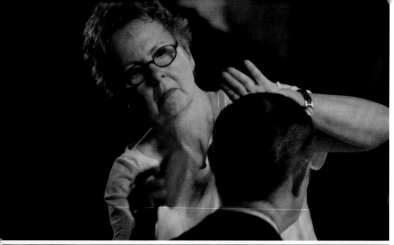

Costume Designer
  Claire Anderson

Hair and Make-up Designer
  Anne 'Nosh' Oldham

Assistant Costume Designer
  Bobbie Edwards

Costume Supervisor
  Beth Lewis

Hair and Make-up Supervisor
  Elaine Browne

David Tennant Personal Hair
and Make-up Artist
  Stevie Smith

Michael Sheen Personal Hair
and Make-up Artist
  Janine Summerhayes

Production Designer
    Michael Ralph

Supervising Art Director
    Mark Hudson

Set Decorator
    Bronwyn Franklin

Art Director
    Martin Boddison

Production Sound Mixer
    Peter Brill

Composer
    David Arnold

Music Supervisor
    Catherine Grimes

SFX Supervisor
    Danny Hargreaves

Stunt Co-ordinator
    Cedric Proust

Health & Safety Advisor
    Sudeep Mitra

VFX Editor
    Dan Mcintosh

VFX Producer
    Alan Church

VFX Designer
    Jean-Claude 'JC' Deguara

VFX Producer
    Louise Hastings

VFX On-set Supervisor
    David Jones

Series Casting Director
  Suzanne Smith

Casting Director (SA)
  Christa Schamberger

Series Location Manager
  Nick Marshall

Location Manager (SA)
  Morten Nielsen

Business and Legal Affairs
    Kate Boyle

Financial Controller
    Dave Robbins

GOD: Over the years a huge number of theological man hours have been spent debating the question: *How Many Angels Can Dance on the Head of a Pin?*

GOD: To answer it, we need information. Firstly, angels don't dance. It's one of the distinguishing characteristics that marks an angel. So, none.

At least, nearly none.

GOD: Aziraphale had learned to gavotte in a discreet gentlemen's club in Portland Place, in the late 1880s. After a while he had become fairly good at it, and was quite put out when, some decades later, the gavotte went out of style for good. So providing the dance was a gavotte, the answer is a straightforward: *one*.

GOD: Then again, you might just as well ask how many demons can dance on the head of a pin. They're of the same original stock, after all. And at least demons dance. Not what you'd call good dancing, though.

GOD: But angels and demons aren't bound by physics. If you look from really close up, the only problem about dancing on the head of a pin is all those big gaps between electrons.

ABOUT MATT WHYMAN

Matt Whyman is the award-winning author of novels including *The Savages* and *Boy Kills Man*. He had authorized access to cast and crew on set and location, in the UK and South Africa.

MATT'S ACKNOWLEDGEMENTS

I should like to thank several members of the *Good Omens* crew who took me and helped me to feel like part of the family. Without production manager Kyla Brennan's tireless organizational skills, I would still be sitting alone in a trailer with a blank notebook and empty schedule. My gratitude also goes to second assistant director, Jan Zalar, who never once pretended to be busy when I showed up in the production office.

Thank you also to Sarah Emsley, Frances Edwards, Jennifer Doyle and the team at Headline; Suzy Smithson at Narrativia, Eirwen Davies and Kate Boyle at the BBC, Philippa Milnes-Smith and all at LAW, as well as Emma Tait and Lynne Eve for their fine editorial and design work.

Finally, to Neil Gaiman, Douglas Mackinnon, Rob Wilkins and the cast and crew for being so generous with their time while working tirelessly on a TV series that's as delightful to watch as it has been to witness in the making.

Two writers walk into a bar... Neil and Matt consider the arrival of War on location just outside Cape Town.